COMMERCIAL MEDIATION PRACTICE GUIDE

A Practical Handbook for Lawyers and Their Business Clients

THIRD EDITION

BENNETT G. PICKER AND CONNA A. WEINER

ABA
AMERICAN BAR ASSOCIATION
Dispute Resolution Section

Cover design by Mary Anne Kulchawik/ABA Design

Printed in the United States of America.

26 25 24 23 5 4 3 2 1

Library of Congress Cataloging-in-Publication Data

Names: Picker, Bennett G., 1941- author. | Weiner, Conna A., author. | American Bar Association. Section of Dispute Resolution, sponsoring body.
Title: Commercial mediation practice guide : a practical handbook for lawyers and their business clients / Bennett G. Picker, Esq. and Conna A. Weiner, Esq.
Description: Third edition. | Chicago, Illinois : American Bar Association, [2022] | Includes bibliographical references and index. | Summary: "This book is intended to serve as a practical guide to assist both lawyers and non-lawyer business executives in effectively navigating and succeeding in the landscape of commercial mediation. This third edition of the Commercial Mediation Practice Guide continues to offer the reader a user friendly guide to the process of mediation and offers checklists wherever possible"-- Provided by publisher.
Identifiers: LCCN 2022038259 (print) | LCCN 2022038260 (ebook) | ISBN 9781639052349 (hardback) | ISBN 9781639052356 (ebook)
Subjects: LCSH: Dispute resolution (Law)--United States. | Mediation--United States. | Conflict management--United States.
Classification: LCC KF9084 .P53 2022 (print) | LCC KF9084 (ebook) | DDC 347.73/9--dc23/eng/20221110
LC record available at https://lccn.loc.gov/2022038259
LC ebook record available at https://lccn.loc.gov/2022038260

Discounts are available for books ordered in bulk. Special consideration is given to state bars, CLE programs, and other bar-related organizations. Inquire at Book Publishing, ABA Publishing, American Bar Association, 321 N. Clark Street, Chicago, Illinois 60654-7598.

www.shopABA.org

Contents

About the Authors

Ben Picker

Bennett Picker has an active, full-time alternative dispute resolution (ADR) practice, serving both as a mediator and an arbitrator in business disputes and as a trainer in mediation and negotiations. He has successfully resolved many hundreds of domestic and international disputes with a cumulative value of several billion dollars. He has served as a mediator in complex business disputes in corporate and commercial transactions, asset/stock purchase agreements, securities, employment, environmental, Employee Retirement Income Security Act, intellectual property, healthcare, real estate, products liability, bankruptcy, construction, class action, professional liability, and shareholder and partnership disputes.

In 2010, Mr. Picker received the American Bar Association (ABA) Lawyer as Problem Solver Award. He was recognized for his "pioneering efforts to change the landscape of dispute resolution in America." He was similarly recognized for his work in mediation and on behalf of diversity and inclusion by the Pennsylvania Bar Association (the Sir Francis Bacon Alternative Dispute Resolution Award in 2015) and the Philadelphia Bar Association (the PNC Achievement Award in 2017).

Mr. Picker is a member of the National Panel of Distinguished Neutrals and the Employment Panel of the International Institute for Conflict Prevention and Resolution (the CPR Institute); a member of the Commercial Mediation (Master Mediator Panel), Arbitration, and National Class Action Panels of the American Arbitration Association (AAA); a fellow of the International Academy of Mediators and is certified by the International Mediation Institute (IMI). He also serves on the mediation panels of the Singapore International Mediation Center, the Florence International Mediation

Center, and the College of Arbitration for Sport (Lausanne, Switzerland). Mr. Picker has served on the Executive Advisory Committee of the CPR Institute, the board of directors and executive committee of the AAA, and also chaired the AAA National Mediation Committee. Mr. Picker has served as a representative of the IMI to the United Nations and as a member of the editorial board of the *Dispute Resolution Journal*.

Mr. Picker was named one of the Top 100 Pennsylvania Super Lawyers consecutively since 2004 by a vote of his peers. In addition, he was selected to be included in the 2005–2022 editions of *The Best Lawyers in America* and was named the Best Lawyers Philadelphia Area Lawyer of the Year for mediation for 10 of the past 15 years.

An active participant in the Philadelphia Bar Association, Mr. Picker served as the Association's chancellor and chair of the Association's board of governors and chair of its judiciary and appellate courts committees. He is a founder and advisory board member of Pennsylvanians for Modern Courts and a former member of the Pennsylvania Trial Court Nominating Commission (First Judicial District).

Mr. Picker received his BA from Temple University, magna cum laude, and his JD from Columbia Law School, where he served as executive editor for the *Columbia Journal of Transnational Law*. He was a partner and is now senior counsel of the Stradley Ronon law firm.

Conna A. Weiner

Conna A. Weiner is a full-time international and U.S. domestic mediator and arbitrator. Her practice is split fairly evenly between these two modalities; her experience in each arena influences the other.

She brings to her U.S. and international mediation and arbitration practice a unique combination of litigation, transactional, and in-house experience after roles with an internationally known law firm and multinational life sciences (pharmaceuticals, medical device, diagnostics, vaccines, and other therapeutics) and healthcare companies. A member of the JAMS panel of mediators and arbitrators, she has extensive experience mediating and arbitrating (in-person and virtually) complex general commercial cases in the United States and internationally, as well as franchise and employment matters, and serves as a sole arbitrator, neutral party–appointed arbitrator on three-member panels, and as the chair of arbitration tribunals under the rules of the major ADR providers, including JAMS, the CPR Institute, the AAA and International Centre for Dispute Resolution, the International

Chamber of Commerce (ICC), the American Health Lawyers Association, and other organizations, as well as non-administered, ad hoc arbitrations using UNCITRAL and other rules. She is also on the World Intellectual Property Organization Panel of Neutrals and the invitation-only Tech List of the Silicon Valley Arbitration and Mediation Center. Her experience in the pharmaceutical, medical device, diagnostic, and other therapeutics industries is particularly unique and sought after in connection with dispute resolution clause requirements requiring therapeutics or related industry experience.

Although she has decades of experience in general commercial and employment matters, representing both plaintiffs and defendants, and is noted for her ability to help parties assess their positions before and after litigations or arbitrations are filed, Ms. Weiner's extensive transactional and deal work over the years help her rapidly appreciate the core issues involved in business arbitrations and mediations and creatively assist parties in structuring an appropriate arbitration process or working out negotiated business solutions that help preserve relationships. Her inside counsel experience helps her understand and communicate with clients and maintain an objective perspective in connection with a wide variety of matters.

Ms. Weiner has special expertise in the full range of unique, complex legal issues and contractual arrangements prevalent in life sciences (such as intellectual property, licensing and acquisitions, supply agreements and the research, development and commercialization of pharmaceuticals, medical devices, and diagnostics), healthcare (both payors and providers), and other technology arenas.

Ms. Weiner is a Fellow in the Chartered Institute of Arbitrators and holds a number of leadership positions in legal and dispute resolution organizations. She is a previous co-chair of the Women in Dispute Resolution (WIDR) Committee of the ABA Section on Dispute Resolution where she initiated through WIDR and with the help of many other ABA members, as well as the support of ABA leadership in the Dispute Resolution Section, the passage of Resolution 105, the resolution urging increased diversity in the ADR profession. She is a graduate of Oberlin College, with highest honors, with a BA in Government and Dance, and the University of Chicago Law School.

Introduction and Acknowledgments

This book is intended to serve as a practical guide to assist both lawyers and non-lawyer business executives in effectively navigating and succeeding in the landscape of commercial mediation.

Mediation is a powerful tool to resolve business disputes early, cost-effectively, and fairly. Of course, mediation should not be thought of as a substitute for strong trial skills and good preparation. However, in the appropriate case—and even in situations before a litigation or arbitration is filed—mediation offers a more direct, less risky, and less costly path toward a flexible, business-friendly resolution. A skilled mediator can work with parties to a dispute to facilitate communication, to assure that the parties are making realistic risk assessments, and to explore the potential for business-driven solutions. Many of these solutions are simply unavailable in the "win-lose" environment of litigation or arbitration.

This third edition of *Commercial Mediation Practice Guide* continues to offer the reader a user-friendly guide to the process of mediation and offers checklists wherever possible. However, in the almost two decades since the last edition, the landscape of mediation has grown and changed dramatically, and we have to some extent narrowed, definitely expanded, and significantly updated this edition to reflect these developments.

First, we have chosen in this edition to focus exclusively on the mediation of business disputes—hence the change in the title of this edition to *Commercial Mediation*—given the many developments in this field and the specialized issues related to, for example, the mediation of employment disputes (which we do not address here). In addition, since commercial mediation has become widely accepted, less advocacy for the process itself is necessary as counsel and parties have grown to appreciate the benefits of mediation.

Recognizing that mediation advocates have become more sophisticated users of the process, we have gone into greater depth covering key preparation and advanced practice topics. Moreover, as the process of mediation has changed over the past two decades, we have treated many topics differently such as, for example, the extent to which the joint session has begun to disappear, the process has required a greater use of evaluative techniques, and ways in which mediators can help participants overcome their cognitive biases and illusions. We also emphasize the effectiveness of mediating before a litigation or arbitration is filed so long as certain best practices are followed, and, throughout, the importance of preparation—indeed, the idea that mediation should be viewed not as "the day" but rather as a process that starts with the planning call, moves through preparation steps and also includes in-person session(s).

We have also added a number of topics and sections not covered in the earlier edition, such as **best practices for virtual mediation**, the development of which has been driven by the pandemic and revolutionized the field; **dispute avoidance or prevention** as opposed to resolution, concepts long accepted and developed in the construction field and complex collaborations in such industries as the life sciences; best practices for **mediating before an arbitration or litigation is filed**; the **importance of diversity in the profession** and steps that can be taken to achieve greater diversity; corporate and law firm dispute prevention and resolution strategies; **deal mediation**; the use of **standby neutrals**; **co-mediation**; the **role of insurance representatives** in mediation; **intellectual property disputes**; and **multiple-party and class action mediations**. We include a number of new business case studies based upon actual disputes, particularly in the life sciences and healthcare.

Finally, as the new title also suggests, we have offered the reader the insights we have gained coming to the process from two different worlds. While we both have decades of experience as lawyers and litigators, as well as mediators, one of us came to mediation as a litigator in complex business disputes and the other as a former litigator and corporate inside counsel who became a transactional/business counselor as well. To that end, we have highlighted the **important role that non-lawyer business executives can and should play** in mediations—with a new chapter (chapter 8) devoted entirely to that subject.

Lawyer advocates and business executives who are familiar with the process will be well prepared to add value to their clients. It is our hope that this practice guide will contribute meaningfully to these efforts.

This introduction would not be complete without acknowledging the tremendous support over the years that we each have received from our friends and colleagues in the dispute resolution community, Ben from his law firm, and from our families as we work to balance responsibilities on the home and work fronts. One of the joys of working in this field is the commitment of neutrals to advancing the field. We hope that through this book we are giving back to the community and to our mediation clients—we learn from all of them every day.

Chapter 1
Mediation and the Landscape of Commercial Dispute Resolution

1.1 Introduction

In the decades since the first edition of this book was published, the meaning of the acronym *ADR* largely has changed from *alternative dispute resolution* to *appropriate dispute resolution*, or simply *dispute resolution*. The non-litigation methods of dispute resolution are increasingly accepted—they are no longer merely alternative. Mediation in the United States has become so commonplace in business disputes that some wonder whether it has become a substitute for litigation itself. In 2013, the largest arbitration provider in the United States, the American Arbitration Association (AAA), updated its rules to include, among other things, a rule that requires parties to mediate cases above a certain dollar amount or to opt out of the process.[1] The value of the mediation in commercial disputes received a significant international vote of confidence with the passage of the Singapore Mediation Convention that is referenced later in this chapter.

Although arbitration clearly has a significant and appropriate role in dispute resolution, it often suffers from the same limitations as litigation—it is rights-based and, without careful management by the parties, counsel, and the arbitration tribunal, it can become as costly and time consuming as litigation. Indeed, when appropriate controls are missing, arbitration is sometimes derisively referred to as "litigation lite." As a consequence, not only are parties increasingly turning to voluntary mediation as a means of resolving business disputes, but court systems and governmental agencies are mandating mediation. Some states are amending their rules of professional conduct to require the consideration of mediation. In the appropriate scenario, lawyers and clients find mediation to be *the* most powerful tool to resolve business disputes early, cost effectively, and fairly.

With the advent of the COVID-19 pandemic in March 2020, virtual mediations that were conducted by using a number of different platforms revolutionized how mediations are performed. Virtual mediation options made the process in general—and early mediation in particular—even more cost effective and flexible. We outline suggested best practices in section 3.3.3 of this guide.

Indeed, before a lawsuit or arbitration is even filed, parties are continuing to develop and explore the notion of dispute prevention through the use of

---

1. American Arbitration Association, Commercial Arbitration Rules and Mediation Procedures, http://www.adr.org/sites/default/files/CommercialRules_Web-Final.pdf (last visited Aug. 10, 2022).

party-directed contractual mechanisms and third-party neutrals in real time, rather than after a *dispute* becomes a *Dispute*, or worse, a *Claim*.

Ultimately, mediation has dramatically changed the landscape of dispute resolution in our society. As a consequence, in virtually every case, lawyers need to determine whether a dispute should be resolved by negotiation, litigation, or mediation, or by some other form of dispute resolution. To provide clients with the benefit of dispute resolution counseling and advocacy at sophisticated levels, lawyers who are engaged in dispute resolution and litigation need to become fully acquainted with the process of mediation.

In addition, we believe that the parties to business disputes, especially non-lawyer business executives who regularly engage in the negotiation and implementation of contracts with external business partners, must also become familiar with the various forms of dispute resolution, and in particular, mediation. Good negotiation skills and focusing on business solutions rather than merely winning are keys to success in mediation. Keeping the focus on a business solution can help keep the dispute from escalating further. Virtual mediation has made it easier than ever for multiple business executives who are managing their bottom line and business objectives to stay front and center in the process and to keep a business focus. It is for these reasons that we have specifically called out non-lawyer business clients as a key audience for this revised guide.

1.2 Commercial Mediation Defined

At its most basic, mediation is a process that employs a neutral person—the mediator—to facilitate and guide negotiations between parties to a dispute in an effort to reach a mutually acceptable resolution. Mediations are:

- Voluntary
- Flexible
- Confidential
- Informal
- Non-binding

Unlike an arbitrator or a judge, a mediator does not—indeed, they cannot—impose a solution on the parties to a dispute. A mediator also does not give the parties legal advice. Instead, a mediator works with the parties to assist them in defining their objectives and achieving a resolution of their differences. Although mediation is a non-binding process, the result of this process in the vast majority of cases is an agreement that is both binding and enforceable.

Mediation has been used in many settings over the years, including in divorce and family law, and in employment, consumer, and commercial settings. This book focuses on commercial mediation—namely, on the mediation of disputes between and among individuals or entities that are engaged in the huge variety of business arrangements involved in, for example, discovering, financing, building, manufacturing, protecting, and selling real estate, goods, and services.

In the commercial mediation process, although a mediator can never impose a solution, we have found that it is almost always expected that the mediator will go beyond what might be perceived as merely facilitating communications between the parties and actively engage in guiding the parties realistically to evaluate their chances of success in a litigation or arbitration. And a mediator is expected to help the businesses consider alternative business arrangements as part of an amicable way forward. Because of this, in certain cases, some familiarity with similar transactions or industry issues on the part of the mediator is considered critical, or at least helpful, by the mediating parties.

Mediation often redefines the way parties view a dispute by looking beyond positional bargaining over issues such as who "breached" and the extent of a party's "damages." The process creates an opportunity to explore underlying business interests, examine the relationships between parties to a dispute, and "fix" problems that arose in the course of the implementation of an external partnership. A skilled mediator, therefore, can help the parties overcome hostilities and legal posturing. A mediator often can develop creative, business-driven solutions that go beyond or replace payments to the aggrieved party. For example, claims for breaches of distributorship agreements have been settled by redefining territorial limits. Termination of a multi-year research, development, and commercialization agreement for a life sciences product has been accompanied by a renegotiated, narrower agreement that focuses on aspects of the collaboration that worked and the payment of software maintenance fees that permit the continued use of a jointly developed program. Claims for breaches of agreements between vendor and vendee have been settled by agreements on future price discounts. In disputes between partners or shareholders who are also members of the same family, apologies have served as the linchpin of settlements. As these examples demonstrate, mediation offers the potential for a win-win solution in contrast to arbitration and litigation, in which there is a winner and a loser. But even in a "pure dollars" dispute, a mediator can facilitate communications, assist the parties in making a realistic assessment of their case, and help structure creative means of monetary exchange.

Another important feature of commercial mediation—arising in part from the potential of a business solution other than only the exchange of money—is the importance, and indeed the prominence, of business client participation, including inside counsel if available, but also non-lawyer business executives and those involved in the creation or implementation of the business arrangement that is the source of the dispute. In addition, outside counsel participants may need to include attorneys other than litigators. For example, outside counsel may need to include transactional counsel to assist with drafting. In some cases, as the negotiations go on, the litigator, having prepared the client with an assessment of the risks and discussion of the cost of an adjudicated process, does not necessarily need to continue to participate directly and can take a step back.

Businesses also are increasingly using mediation to resolve disputes early, including before a litigation or arbitration is filed. We discuss how best to operate in this setting throughout this book. As we discuss in more detail, early mediation avoids escalating, exacerbating, and possibly expanding the scope of the dispute—through the assertion of counterclaims, for example. In the case of litigation, early mediation avoids a public airing of a fight between business partners.

1.3 Mediation As Facilitated Negotiation: Advantages Over Direct Negotiations Between the Parties

Throughout this book, we advocate that business partners should always attempt to negotiate amicable resolutions of their disputes before turning to help from a third party, be it a legal advocate or a neutral. Simply put, business people know their business needs and interests the best, and they often are quite experienced and skilled in the art of negotiation.

However, when differences persist, at a certain point, parties will start to experience frustration and difficulty in direct settlement negotiations. In addition to the inherent problems arising from the fact that the parties in a negotiation have opposing views and conflicting goals, other issues, such as personal antagonisms, make the process of communication difficult. Involving a mediator usually changes the dynamics of unsuccessful direct negotiations for the better.

Understanding why this is so requires appreciating two important distinctions between direct negotiators and a third-party mediator. The first is that the mediator is a neutral party and trained to maintain that neutrality by understanding and holding both sides of the dispute in their minds simultaneously. The second is that the mediator is new to the dispute. As a result, the mediator is better situated to help the parties take a fresh look at seemingly intractable issues and raise devil's advocate questions about a parties' assessment of the facts, contract language, and law. Once parties reach an impasse in their direct negotiations, they may feel that they have gone over the same ground again and again, and they distrust any suggestions from what has become "the other side." (This psychological phenomenon has a name—*reactive devaluation*—and we discuss it and other barriers to settlement in Chapter 5.)

A skilled mediator can capitalize on their position as a neutral party and help the parties take a fresh look at the dispute and enhance the process of communication and negotiation by:

- Focusing on preparation—for example, by helping the parties fill information gaps and explain their positions to each other and to the mediator
- Managing the agenda
- Clarifying misunderstandings
- Reducing tension
- Framing or reframing issues
- Exploring new areas of discussion
- Helping parties make realistic assessments of both their chances of success in an arbitration or mediation and, with industry expertise, their best way forward for the business in a two-track assessment—by predicting how a judge or arbitrator might resolve the dispute, by using experience in the industry, or with similar facts and legal issues to help evaluate the dispute
- Setting the pace of negotiations
- Making suggestions about who should talk to whom to advance the discussion productively (for example, business-to-business, inside counsel only, or outside counsel only)
- Coaching the parties on moves in negotiations and understanding negotiation norms, such as the difficulty of perceived backsliding and the importance of reciprocity

- Making suggestions for mutually acceptable solutions that go beyond a pure dollars solution
- Ensuring fairness in the process

A mediator typically accomplishes these objectives by meeting with all parties and their counsel, in joint meetings and in separate caucuses as may be appropriate. Increasingly, and particularly in more complex commercial mediations, these sessions can happen over time and in different formats, with large teams or in smaller groups, all facilitated by the ability of parties to meet virtually as we discuss further on. In contrast to direct negotiations between the parties, or even litigation settlement conferences, a mediator usually will respectfully insist on the involvement and presence of representatives of the parties who have ultimate decision-making authority, or at least on assurances that important stakeholders have been involved in assessing settlement options and will be available in the course of the mediation process to discuss them as the negotiations proceed.

1.4 Mediation and Facilitation Compared

Facilitation has no absolute definition, but it can be distinguished from mediation by a decreased importance of the process ending in an agreement to resolve a dispute. Faciliation focuses instead on improving communication and understanding among participants in the facilitated event. The events can be a relatively routine business meeting; a series of curated discussions among business partners who are kicking off a joint venture or trying to diagnose why a collaboration is not working; or meetings of community groups with different views on difficult subjects. One organization, Essential Partners, formerly the Public Conversation Project, uses the term *dialogue* to describe the process it implements, during which it expects particpants to "listen to understand" rather than to achieve an agreement. Before a facilitation session, facilitors often conduct interviews of participants to help shape the agenda and understand the points of difference.[2]

Mediators may use some of the same techniques as facilitators to lay the groundwork for in-person mediation sessions, and the skills of a mediator can be very helpful in a facilitator. Additional resources regarding facilitation are available in our bibliography.

---

2. Essential Partners, What We Do, https://whatisessential.org/our-method (last visited Aug. 10, 2022).

1.5 Mediation and Adjudication Compared: The Litigation Mindset

It is important to understand the distinctions between the characteristics of mediation and those of adjudicative forums (arbitration and litigation). The following chart summarizes the major differences:

Mediation	**Adjudication**
• Parties retain control over outcome.	• Parties relinquish control to third party.
• Neutral assists parties in defining issues and exploring interests and possible resolutions.	• Arbitrator/judge listens to evidence and renders decision.
• Scope of potential compromises is determined by the parties.	• Little potential for creative compromise—decisions made based upon facts and law, for example, remedies limited to damages and injunctions.
• Negotiation is facilitated or guided.	• Outcome is determined.
• Need for information exchange is minimized and focused on key information.	• Discovery often is extensive.
• Process is private and confidential.	• Arbitrations are private (but decisions often available); court hearings and trials are public.
• Parties are encouraged to communicate with each other directly.	• All communications are through lawyer to tribunal.
• Focus is on all logically relevant factors, including issues, interests, emotions, goals, and relationships.	• Focus is narrow and limited by defined set of rules and procedures.
• Joint and individual caucus meetings are informal.	• Hearings are formal and evidentiary.
• Outcome is based upon perceptions and business needs of parties.	• Decisions are based upon evidence and law.
• Parties often agree to mutually satisfactory resolution of dispute, preserving relationships.	• Result makes one party a winner, the other a loser.
• Issues in complex dispute can be telescoped in hours or days.	• Often takes months or years to resolve complex dispute; in litigation, appeals make the process even longer.
• Participants have flexibility to determine ground rules.	• Participants have little or no flexibility—process governed by one set of rules for all parties.
• Process is low-risk and cost effective.	• Arbitration costs are usually higher, and litigation costs are significantly higher.

In a number of places in this book, we refer to the litigation mindset as a potential hindrance to success in mediation. Simply put, the skills required for success in litigation are often different, or of different emphasis, than those that will be more likely to result in a negotiated outcome. A lawyer who is locked in the battle of litigation must adopt an adversarial stance, focus on winning, and tightly control access to her client and witnesses, the flow of information to the "other side," and the rules-driven choreography of the litigation process. A lawyer with such a perspective on a dispute will be wary of compromise, voluntarily sharing information, crediting the other side's perspective in any way, or a more relaxed approach to communications between and among counsel and clients who are managed, to a significant extent, by someone else—namely, by the mediator. The list of differences between mediation and adjudication highlights why lawyers must be prepared to be flexible in their approach to solving the problems of their clients as they look to mediation. Businesspeople who are skilled in negotiation can help their lawyers in this regard by keeping their business needs and interests top of mind.

1.6 A Note on Conciliation

The concept of conciliation is closely related to mediation and definitions differ depending on the jurisdiction. Internationally, conciliation often is said to involve more active participation by the neutral, to the extent that the conciliator will make settlement proposals for the parties to assess and drive the process forward in an evaluative way. Because the definitions of this process differ widely and sometimes are so closely related to a highly evaluative mediation style, we will not address this in further detail and instead list resources in our bibiliography for further reading.

1.7 Mediation, Dispute Prevention, and Dispute Resolution

Many practitioners have moved away from using the phrase *alternative dispute resolution* and toward using the broader possibility of *appropriate* dispute resolution, or simply, dispute resolution. There is also a focus on preventing disputes from arising in the first place. This is referred to as *dispute avoidance*, *dispute prevention*, and the like, and they often developed out of concepts arising in the construction industry in the 1990s. Whatever the phrase that is used to describe the alternatives to an adjudicated solution, it is important to consider all options and to remember that the skills and techniques of a mediator can be helpful at many stages, including dispute prevention.

Moreover, these alternatives should not be regarded as mutually exclusive. Litigation can and should remain on the table for the right reasons if it is consistent with business goals and efficiency. In some circumstances, for example, a focused litigation strategy can promote a favorable outcome in mediation (for example, when the parties need a legal response to drive an amicable resolution) and provide a forum in the event that a mediation is unsuccessful.

Mediation and binding arbitration are clearly the two leading approaches to resolving disputes that have developed to the point of considering an adjudication alternative. In this book, we focus on the core skills and principles involved in using a third-party neutral to help resolve disputes—consistent with the definition of mediation set forth above.

However, there are a number of non-traditional approaches to dispute prevention and dispute resolution, some of which rely upon the parties themselves, use a mediator's skills, or encompass many of the same features presented by mediation, especially privacy, confidentiality, and the opportunity for prompt resolution. Among these approaches are the following, which we have roughly divided between avoidance/prevention and resolution.

Dispute Avoidance or Prevention

- Partnering (for example, in the mid-1990's, the U.S. government began requiring in a request for proposal [RFP] that the contractor commit to formal management procedures that reflect cooperation and teamwork so that claims and conflict are reduced or eliminated.)
- Facilitation (see section 1.4)
- Alliance management/relationship manager
- Deal mediation (see special topics in chapter 9)
- Standby; standing mediator (see special topics in chapter 9)
- Dispute resolution boards: Advisory opinions

Dispute Resolution

- Early neutral evaluation (written opinion issued by a neutral)
- Dispute resolution boards: Final rulings
- Mediation–arbitration (med–arb) (see section 1.9)
- Mock arbitrations (one or three arbitrators are presented with arguments, and arbitrators issue opinions and/or comment on the evidence; can be retained by one side or both sides on a confidential basis)

- Non-binding arbitration (an advisory opinion that is not enforceable is sought)
- High–low arbitration (arbitrator restricted to an award within a range)
- Baseball arbitration (arbitrator must choose one or another number, or one or another party's statement of the issues; theory is that it makes the proposals more reasonable and achieves an efficient result)
- Mini-trial
- Multi-party coordinated defense

Sophisticated parties are increasingly looking at the full range of dispute prevention and dispute resolution options short of a full-blown litigation so that they can get back to business. Our bibliography lists selected references regarding some of the non-mediation alternatives discussed here.

1.8 The Online and Virtual Mediation Revolution

The COVID-19 pandemic touched off nothing short of a revolution in how mediation was practiced during the pandemic and likely has permanently changed the mediation landscape. Simply put, virtual mediation on platforms such as Zoom is widely accepted in the mediation community and by users, and, if done right, has many advantages over in-person sessions.

For many years, thoughtful practitioners have developed the theory and practice of online dispute resolution (ODR). M. Ethan Katsch and Janet Rifkin call technology *the fourth party* to a dispute in their seminal 2001 book *Online Dispute Resolution*.[3] Broadly stated, ODR involves the use of online communication tools, either asynchronous (not in real time, such as email) or synchronous (in real time, such as video conferencing) to assist in the resolution of disputes.

ODR has been particularly prominent in connection with e-commerce disputes, such as the resolution of disputes between buyers and sellers on eBay, and now Airbnb, Uber, and many other online retailers. The development of e-commerce in effect depends on the ability of consumers to quickly and easily reverse transactions in connection with the purchase of items and services that they cannot physically see, or in the case of eBay, in dealings with strangers. The European Union has been very active in encouraging the use of ODR in connection with online retailer–consumer disputes

3. M. Ethan Katsch & Janet Rifkin, Online Dispute Resolution (2001).

by requiring it of retailers within its jurisdiction pursuant to its European Online Dispute Resolution platform.[4]

ODR technology became quite sophisticated over the years and moved from administration-based technology to resolution-based technology, using software to assist in formulating a resolution for parties (Smartsettle and Cybersettle for insurance disputes). In his 2002 book, *Online Dispute Resolution for Business*, Colin Rule describes some of the basic tools that were available at that time: email, discussion environments such as listservs, instant messaging, chat rooms, audio conferencing and video conferencing, along with software permitting automated negotiation, solution-set databases, and blind bidding or automated arbitration. Rule noted that shortcomings on the Internet were likely to keep videoconferencing of limited utility for quite some time.[5] More generally, as late as 2017, the well-established International ODR Forum, which hosted its first conference in Geneva in 2002, panelists questioned why some courts and the legal profession generally were slow to engage with ODR.[6]

Fast-forward to March 2020, and the dramatic improvement of internet speed and bandwidth; cloud computing; sophisticated online communication platforms; and mobile phone technology, combined with the necessity imposed by the pandemic, telescoped into a matter of months the use and acceptance of streaming and video-based ODR vehicles such as Zoom and Microsoft Teams—previously known to business executives but not necessarily to their outside counsel. Indeed, the now widely adopted term *virtual* to describe online Zoom sessions highlights how closely such ODR technology can resemble face-to-face, in-person sessions compared to no-video technologies.

With careful attention to preparation and other best practices set forth in Chapter 3, virtual mediations on Zoom and similar platforms can in many ways be more effective in connection with commercial disputes than in-person processes. The logistical ease with which mediations can be assembled—the ability to include many more stakeholders, including businesspeople with knowledge of the facts, in the process; the more flexible and efficient structure of the mediation sessions; and the relative lack of

4. European Commission, Online Dispute Resolution, How It Works, https://ec.europa.eu/consumers/odr/main/?event=main.home.howitworks (last visited Aug. 10, 2022).

5. Published by Jossey-Bass in 2002. Subtitle is "B2B, ECommerce, Consumer, Employment, Insurance, and Other Commercial Conflicts."

6. See https://library.iccwbo.org/eai-day1.htm.

formality—can contribute to the ability to get a dispute settled earlier and faster. We have heard from a number of our inside clients either that they are never going back to the assumption that mediations will be in-person (in fact, an in-person session will need to be justified in terms of cost and distraction) or, at the very least, whether a mediation will proceed virtually or in-person will be an important strategic decision.

1.9 Mediation–Arbitration (Med–Arb)

In a med–arb proceeding, parties agree in advance that any issues unresolved in mediation will be resolved in binding arbitration by a neutral serving in the dual role of mediator and arbitrator. Parties opting for a single neutral to perform both roles often do so in an effort to save costs. Suffice it to say that the prospective role of arbitrator gives the mediator considerable clout in attempting to forge a settlement. On the other hand, significant advantages may be lost in this scenario because parties are less likely to be candid with the mediator about weaknesses in their case. For this reason, some mediators will not serve in the dual role of mediator and arbitrator. Other mediators will attempt to minimize the use of caucuses so that all parties are aware of what has been shared with the mediator. At the conclusion of a mediation, however, mediators often are willing to serve as an arbitrator to decide minor unresolved issues or issues arising in connection with future related disputes. In all these situations, it is critical to ensure that parties and their counsel are proceeding with fully informed consent, including the risk that the parties will not be as open with the mediator because they will not know the extent to which their confidences may influence an arbitration result when the mediator switches hats.

When parties agree—by contract or otherwise—to mediation followed by binding arbitration using separate neutrals, this two-step procedure does not present the same issues as a true med–arb proceeding. While this two-step procedure is more costly (if the mediation is unsuccessful), it is our view the parties are likely to be far more open with the mediator, and the chances of success in mediation will be greater.

Although even the most experienced litigators ask about binding mediation, there is no such process. The phrase is confusing because it suggests that the parties can be forced to accept an externally imposed resolution of their dispute. It is the voluntarily participatory nature of mediation that creates the bright line that distinguishes mediation from arbitration. Similarly, it would be inappropriate to use the phrase *binding mediation* to refer to a binding commitment to mediate arising from an obligation created by contract or by the court. Of course, a successful mediation can result in a legally binding settlement.

The Mixed Mode Task Force, a joint effort of the College of Commercial Arbitrators, International Mediation Institute, and the Straus Institute for Dispute Resolution at Pepperdine School of Law, has been developing model standards and criteria for ways to combine different dispute resolution processes, including assessing the notion that mediators can set the stage for arbitration (a concept we strongly endorse), the idea that arbitrators can serve as mediators or set the stage for settlement, and other concepts.[7]

1.10 Dispute Prevention and Resolution Clauses in Contracts

Parties in industries that feature long-term, complex collaborations, such as construction or the life sciences, have long used sophisticated dispute avoidance or prevention mechanisms to prevent serious disputes from arising in the first place (and therefore avoiding additional mediation, arbitration, or litigation to resolve). These techniques—often memorialized in contracts that also include more traditional dispute resolution clauses—include partnering, party alliance management, committee structures to manage governance, real-time involvement of third-party neutrals such as standing mediators and dispute resolution boards on an advisory basis, and other mechanisms written into agreements.

By force of necessity, the construction industry has been a leader in dispute avoidance or prevention techniques. Simply put, pausing the construction of an airport in order to run to court to resolve payment disputes is just not a viable option. For example, in the mid-1990's, the U.S. General Services Administration began requiring as part of its RFP process that contractors commit to a team-based, formal management process to reduce or eliminate conflict and claims that widely became known as partnering. The construction industry has also been at the forefront of the development and use of dispute advisory boards or dispute resolution boards—groups of knowledgeable neutrals who are retained at the beginning of the project, learn the parameters, and are available in real time to give advisory or final opinions so that projects are not derailed.

7. See https://imimediation.org/about/who-are-imi/mixed-mode-task-force/.

The pharmaceutical and IT industries have long employed the use of *alliance managers*, or relationship managers, to help troubleshoot issues in collaborations. These are not neutrals but rather, employees of the entities that are involved in the collaboration. An entire organization, the Association of Strategic Alliance Professionals, was created to serve as a platform for discussing various issues and provides a certification program.

The International Institute for Conflict Prevention and Resolution (the CPR Institute) has recently begun highlighting dispute prevention and has promulgated a dispute prevention pledge, discussed further later in the book.

For those disputes that do need to be raised and resolved more formally, parties to written agreements are paying greater attention to the more standard dispute resolution clause in contracts. Traditionally, it has been common for lawyers to insert an arbitration clause in a contract in which parties to an agreement prefer arbitration to litigation. However, parties to written agreements are increasingly insisting on progressive, multi-step contract clauses that require, for example, executive negotiations followed by mediation followed by arbitration. (In this book, we address some of the skepticism about contractually required mediation. We think that it generally is a very good idea, if it's implemented appropriately.)

In some circumstances, parties to a written agreement may prefer mediation as a predicate to the trigger of litigation. In other circumstances, especially where a party anticipates a large volume of small-dollar disputes, when the paramount interest is minimizing legal and transactional costs, or in a cross-border transaction [where global enforceability of the award pursuant to the 1958 New York Convention (https://www.newyorkconvention.org) and a neutral international panel are always critical considerations], a party may prefer mediation followed by arbitration. (For a more detailed explanation of factors favoring and weighing against mediation, see section 2.2.)

Multi-step—or *waterfall*—clauses that require negotiation, mediation, and arbitration or litigation must be carefully drafted to ensure that each party's obligations at each step are clear. Is mediation unambiguously required as a condition precedent to arbitration or litigation? Who needs to participate? How long do the parties need to negotiate or mediate before turning to the next step in the clause? What description of the dispute—in the form of a claim notice, for example—or documents should be provided in connection with the negotiation or mediation? Should the applicable statute of limitations be tolled?

In drafting the section of the dispute resolution clause that provides for arbitration, it is important to focus on key issues such as the scope of the agreement to arbitrate, the decision to appoint one or three arbitrators, whether or not party-designated arbitrators are neutral or partisan, limitations on the time between the appointment of the arbitration panel and the award, what kind of discovery or disclosure will be allowed (because the general understanding is that this will be limited in comparison with litigation), continued tolling of the statute of limitations, the need for a carve-out for injunctive relief, the desire for a bare or reasoned award, and the desire to preclude an award for punitive damages.

The major institutional providers, including the AAA, the CPR Institute, JAMS, and for international cases, the International Chamber of Commerce, among others, all have helpful dispute resolution clause language templates and checklists on their websites to ensure that the basic issues are covered. The websites for these providers and others are set forth in our bibliography.

1.11 Mediation in Complex Litigation: Cooperative Case Management

Mediation is most often thought of as an alternative to litigation. However, we are beginning to see an innovative form of mediation *within* the framework of litigation. Multiparty cases, complex cases, and even more so, mass disaster cases, offer opportunities for this form of mediation—the mediation of differences among and between parties in litigation. In many such cases, cooperation in the initial stages of litigation is difficult because many defendants seek to minimize their own exposure and to maximize the responsibility and exposure of co-defendants. In complex cases involving multiple defendants, the pursuit of crossclaims and the inability to cooperate can often be prescriptions for disaster.

Defendants in such cases can achieve significant benefits by jointly retaining a mediator (or facilitator) to work with all defendants toward common goals such as (1) entering into a joint or cooperative defense agreement; (2) removing crossclaims from the court system to an agreed-upon process of alternative dispute resolution; and (3) coordinating cooperation in discovery, motion practice, and preparation for trial.

As one example, in cooperation with the CPR Institute, a mediator was able to achieve some or all of these benefits on behalf of the more than 40 "product and service" defendants in the One Meridian Plaza Fire litigation in Philadelphia, on behalf of the product defendants in the Happy Land

Social Club Fire litigation in New York, and on behalf of defendants in the Dupont Plaza Hotel Fire litigation in San Juan, Puerto Rico.

Among the benefits that can be achieved as the result of a cooperative defense agreement are the following:

- Informal discovery among and between defendants
- Joint efforts to build a defense
- Joint fact investigations
- Jointly retained experts
- Cooperation among experts
- Cooperation in formal discovery
- Exploration of global settlement possibilities
- Savings on transcripts, document management, and other costs

A cooperative litigation management strategy must take into account the inherent conflict between target defendants and peripheral defendants. The parties also must address the difficult issues that surround the desire of a party to control the litigation as well as legal issues involving work product and privilege. With the assistance of a skilled mediator, most of the difficult issues can be resolved to the satisfaction of the participating parties.

Defendants in complex and multiparty cases can achieve important strategic advantages and significant savings through cooperation and the use of a mediator. In coming years, we are likely to see this innovative form of mediation used with increasing frequency.

1.12 International Mediation

There have been a number of important efforts internationally to encourage commerical mediation, all reflecting the greatly increased acceptance of the process. A survey of those developments is beyond the scope of this book, but a few developments deserve mention, and our bibliography provides additional resources.

In 2008, the European Union published its Directive on Mediation. The objective of the Directive was to "facilitate access to alternative dispute resolution and to promote the amicable settlement of disputes by encouraging the use of mediation and by ensuring a balanced relationship between mediation and judicial proceedings" (Preamble). Further information regarding the status of the Directive and its effect can be found in the bibliography.

Furthermore, on September 12, 2020, the United Nations Convention on International Settlement Agreements Resulting from Mediation, commonly refered to as the Singapore Mediation Convention, entered into force. As of this writing, 53 countries, including the United States, have signed the convention.[8]

The Singapore Mediation Convention preamble explicitly notes the value for international trade of mediation as a method for settling commercial disputes in which the parties in dispute request a third person or persons to assist them in their attempt to settle the dispute amicably. It also notes that mediation is increasingly used in international and domestic commercial practice as an alternative to litigation and recites the benefits of mediation. Signatories to the convention are required to enforce international mediated settlement agreements in accordance with the rules of the Convention. The Convention explicitly does not apply to settlement agreements relating to consumer, family, inheritance, or employment law (Convention Article 2).

The Singapore Mediation Convention, along with the EU Directive on Mediation and similar developments around the world, are important developments in mediation practice and reflect the growing use of mediation internationally in connection with commercial agreements.[9]

8. See https://eur-lex.europa.eu/legal-content/EN/TXT/?uri=celex%3A32008L0052 and https://www.singaporeconvention.org.

9. See https://www.singaporeconvention.org/convention/text.

Chapter 2
The Decision to Mediate

2.1 Introduction

The decision to mediate often is driven by the general advantages of mediation discussed in the preceding chapter. When drafting a dispute resolution clause in a written agreement, counsel should examine whether mediation is likely to advance the client's interests given the kinds of disputes most likely to arise (see section 1.10). In the absence of a written agreement, each particular dispute must be examined by each party on its own merits to determine whether mediation is the best alternative. This chapter discusses the key issues in making the decision to mediate—whether to mediate, when to mediate, why mediation succeeds or fails, and how to propose mediation.

In addition, with the advent of virtual mediation, an important strategic decision is whether or not to insist on an in-person mediation or whether instead to proceed virtually or on a hybrid basis.

2.2 Suitability of Dispute for Mediation

2.2.1 Introduction

In every dispute, counsel should consider whether a client's objectives can best be achieved through negotiation, mediation, arbitration, litigation, or some other form of alternative dispute resolution. While mediation is not one-size-fits-all, we believe that the benefits and disadvantages of mediation should be discussed with the client in virtually every business dispute.

Not every case is appropriate for mediation. In some cases, mediation is not necessary to achieve a negotiated resolution. Parties often overlook the possibility of resolving a dispute through direct and unassisted negotiations—an option that should be examined in every case (see chapter 5). In other cases, litigation may be the best dispute resolution alternative. For example, in an intellectual property dispute, a patent holder may want to establish the meets and bounds of its property rights publicly and with respect to all potential challengers. There may be an unresolved legal question at the heart of the dispute that needs a court decision. Similarly, litigation may be the best alternative if a party needs injunctive relief or is defending a frivolous lawsuit.

However, most cases that are suitable for a negotiated resolution are also suitable for mediation. This is particularly true if business leader participation is needed to resolve the dispute—and in business disputes, that often is the case. Moreover, a dispute may be ripe for mediation notwithstanding the fact that there have been failed negotiations in the past or the fact that the controversy is the subject of a pending lawsuit. As noted, the involvement of a neutral third party can inspire a fresh look at a dispute with the help of that neutral's questions and guidance.

It is also almost never too early to think about mediation. Some litigators are of the view that they need to show their adversary that they are serious by filing suit, or that they—or both sides—need discovery to assess claims. As discussed in the section below, focusing on early mediation techniques, however, with the right attitude and preparation, the mediator and the parties can use the mediation process to demonstrate the seriousness of their positions and fill information gaps regarding facts and claims. In addition, taking a step into an adjudication process exacerbates conflict and can make it that much harder to achieve an early amicable resolution.

2.2.2 *Factors Favoring Mediation*

Some disputes are particularly suitable for mediation. Factors favoring mediation include:

- Need to avoid publicity/need for confidentiality or privacy
- Desire for speedy resolution/need to avoid delay
- Need to preserve continuing relationships
- Need to terminate a relationship in a manner that recognizes the possibility or inevitability of future relationships
- Recognition that emotions or hostilities may bar a settlement
- Desire to minimize risk of an imposed outcome
- Need to reduce high costs of any litigation, but particularly if the case is complex, technical or multiple-party
- Need for neutral expert help in working out a solution
- Desire to expand possible remedies beyond the win or lose of adjudication to include business solutions such as, in effect, renegotiating a contract
- Desire to avoid adverse precedent
- No need to establish a precedent
- Existence of collateral issues that may enhance resolution in a mediation forum

2.2.3 *Factors Weighing Against Mediation*

The nature of some disputes suggests litigation as the most appropriate dispute resolution alternative. Factors weighing against mediation include:

- Insistence on revenge or injury to a competitor as a goal of the dispute resolution process
- Need to establish a legal precedent
- Absence of a bona fide dispute—other side's case is frivolous
- Entire case likely to be decided on motion to dismiss or motion for summary judgment
- Need for time to elapse before settlement possibilities can be evaluated (for business or legal reasons)

- Other parties are not yet aware of the dispute or have not yet been identified and need to be included for proper resolution of the dispute
- Authorized decision maker is not available
- Current budget limitations prevent serious settlement negotiations
- Settlement was reached in the past, but a party breached the settlement agreement
- Parties absolutely do not want a settlement
- Need for immediate equitable relief

In deciding whether to mediate, parties should also consider the factors that may suggest binding arbitration as the best dispute resolution alternative. These include, among others, the need for prompt resolution, the desire for privacy, the need to minimize litigation costs, the existence of bad faith in prior negotiations, the high probability that a negotiated settlement is unlikely even in a mediation setting, and the absence of any compelling reason to seek relief in a court of law.

2.2.4 *Suitability Screening*

The CPR Institute developed a suitability screen to assist in making the determination of whether a case is appropriate for mediation or some other non-traditional dispute resolution alternative. Some law firms and corporations have also developed their own suitability screens. These screens allow for a more sophisticated analysis than the list of factors provided in the preceding section. Further, many corporations have adopted formal procedures to institutionalize the analysis of suitability issues. For example, some corporations have a designated dispute resolution counsel to monitor all disputes for this purpose. In addition, some corporations require their outside law firms to justify in writing why a dispute is inappropriate for ADR before allowing a dispute to proceed in the normal course, or requiring mediation attempts within 90 days of being retained (see section 9.2).

2.3 Types of Business Disputes Commonly Mediated

Virtually all types of business disputes that are appropriate and ripe for a negotiated resolution can be mediated. Certain types of business disputes have factors that make the dispute particularly suitable for mediation. For example, construction disputes require real-time solutions to avoid project delays. Contract disputes involving continuing relationships between parties often can be resolved by restructuring relationships, something that can only happen in a negotiation or mediation setting, not arbitration or litigation. In some instances, mediation not only offers a process to resolve existing disputes but also promotes better lines of communication, which tend to reduce future problems.

Business disputes that are commonly mediated with success include:

- Bankruptcy and creditor/debtor
- Post-merger and acquisition: milestones/earnouts, purchase price adjustments, etc.
- Joint venture/collaboration disputes (research, development, commercialization of technology or life sciences products, for example)
- Healthcare industry payor–provider disputes
- Real estate transactions
- Software development and implementation projects
- Manufacturing/supply/distribution arrangements
- Investor (individual, private equity, venture capital, shareholder) disputes
- Claims against professionals (lawyers, accountants, etc.)
- Construction
- Franchise
- Environmental
- Insurance coverage
- Intellectual property (licensing, trademark, copyright, patent—inventorship, infringement, validity)
- Partnership
- Regulatory matters
- Securities
- Business torts and unfair competition

2.4 Deciding When to Mediate—and the Advantages of Commencing Mediating Before Any Litigation (the "Filing Effect")

As we have suggested, while every dispute has its own time-related constraints and imperatives, it is generally advisable to mediate a dispute sooner rather than later. Of course, a mediation "too early" in the life of a dispute may be unproductive. The parties may need time to obtain the information necessary for a more meaningful evaluation of the merits of a case. At the same time, parties to disputes routinely resolve their differences through direct, unassisted negotiations without having made a comprehensive investigation of the facts and legal positions. Moreover, even where additional information is necessary in order to make a reasonable evaluation, a mediator can assist the parties in reaching agreements concerning the exchange of information, as we discuss in the chapters on mediation preparation below. When the parties' efforts to achieve a negotiated resolution fail, mediation should be considered as a possible and immediate next step. At this juncture, parties are often still flexible in their positions and are usually interested in the cost savings that will result from avoiding litigation.

In some cases, mediation may be unproductive too early in a dispute because hostilities prevent the parties from communicating effectively. Mediation also may be unproductive because a party, convinced of the correctness of its position, is not prepared to consider an early "compromise"—a barrier to settlement that often is removed once a party incurs substantial costs in litigation. If parties to a dispute wait too long before considering mediation, however, the parties may become too committed to their positions to consider any solution other than litigation.

In fact, the advantages of mediating a dispute before crossing the line into an adjudicative process, be it arbitration or litigation, can be considerable. We have found that many lawyers and their clients consistently underestimate the negative effects of filing an arbitration demand or a complaint on the immediate cost of conflict and the dynamics of the negotiation process. They may think that the "leverage" gained by filing and/or the demonstration of the seriousness and confidence of their client is worth it and insufficiently harmful to think carefully about taking this step.

However, we urge parties to think long and hard about what we call the "filing effect." Litigation expenses can be immediate and significant in the form of document holds, retention of an e-discovery vendor and initial litigation assessments. The business partner now becomes "the other side," and rather than being intimidated, may react with some fury at the escalation of a dispute, harden its position and, with the help of counsel, come up with a retaliatory counterclaim that they would never have asserted if the discussions had remained on a business basis. Indeed, the possibility of counterclaims or defenses relating to the legality of the client's own conduct (from a regulatory or antitrust perspective, for example) must be thoroughly discussed with the client.

Potentially exacerbating this reaction is the change in personnel from the business, transactional and inside counsel to an outside counsel litigation team who will not necessarily bring a business perspective to the dispute and focus, as they must to do their jobs, on who is right and wrong and on vanquishing the other side by winning. Unless parties agree quickly to settlement negotiations, the business loses control over the outcome of the case and the opportunity for flexible, often face-saving business-focused remedies recedes.

In addition, not to be underestimated is the publicity risk associated with litigation (a consideration ameliorated by an agreement to submit a case to arbitration); the business dispute is now public, with the reputational and other potential harms associated with this escalation.

While we have heard some litigators wonder whether the contractually required mediation in a multi-step dispute resolution clause is a waste of time and merely a "check the box" exercise, we think that avoiding these "filing effects," with the critical caveat that parties follow the preparation steps we recommend in this book makes early business mediation worth considering *every* time. If the mediation fails, then both sides are well prepared to take the next step into arbitration or litigation if that is deemed appropriate, perhaps with the issues for consideration considerably narrowed as a result of a robust mediation process.

We have also seen an increasing use of "mediation windows"—a set time in the course of a proceeding when the parties will discuss the possibility of mediation—in arbitrations, either suggested by the arbitrator in the course of setting up the schedule and first procedural order or agreed by the parties themselves. This can very productively remove the hesitation a party may have to suggest mediation during the course of an adjudicated proceeding.

2.5 Why Mediation Works

Most mediations of business disputes are successful because of the following reasons:

- *Greater efficiency*. On many levels, mediation is a highly efficient way of resolving most disputes. Parties often can telescope in days or hours an assessment of the facts and legal issues likely to take months or years to develop in litigation, or arbitration for that matter. (Business clients often are surprised at what it takes to establish facts that seem obvious to them under "evidence" in court, for example.) Information gaps that need to be narrowed in order to understand one's position can be dealt with quickly and relatively informally. As a consequence, parties can avoid substantial costs in legal fees, expense, and indirect costs—time and attention away from the achievement of business objectives—associated with a protracted legal or arbitration action.

- *Interest-based solutions and flexible "remedies."* As the mediator identifies and explores underlying interests and concerns beyond the legal issues and dollar amounts in a dispute, the parties can "enlarge the pie" before dividing it. Parties have the opportunity and incentive to formulate business-driven solutions not available either in court or in arbitration. Agreements that have gone south, for example, can in effect be renegotiated to fix the problems that led the parties to a dispute. A client's desire to avoid a hit to the bottom line in a particular quarter, remove an obstacle to a merger, admit publicly a technical failure or avoid violating a bank covenant all may be addressed in a flexible solution-oriented way that simply is unavailable in litigation or arbitration.
- *Barriers to resolution identified.* Mediation offers an opportunity to identify and overcome potential barriers to a negotiated resolution, such as differing perceptions, mistakes of fact, party problems, issue problems and extrinsic pressures (see section 5.2).
- *More effective communication using a "fresh look."* Mediation gives the parties the opportunity to step back and take a fresh look at their dispute facilitated by a neutral third-party, communicate more effectively and discover common ground through interest-based exploration or other means. In a mediation setting, the parties have an opportunity to speak out on any issue or concern without regard to legal relevance. In a process that is very personal, supported by a neutral, parties develop a sense of investment in the outcome and are more open to changing their perceptions about a dispute when they listen to the other side.
- *Dropping a "Litigation Mindset."* As a corollary to the above, mediation participants are encouraged to stop focusing on a past assessment of who was right and wrong, holding back information for strategic advantage or maintaining positions or postures, and instead focus on forward-looking business solutions.
- *Control by parties.* Participants in mediation have control of not only the outcome but also the process. The process is flexible and can be designed in the manner best suited to achieve a client's goals and objectives (e.g., limited discovery or no discovery, with or without written submissions, with controlled exchanges by experts where advisable).

- *Privacy and confidentiality.* The private and confidential nature of the process allows for more open communications than in arbitration or litigation (see section 6.9), which enhances the possibility of settlement. Parties are less reluctant to disclose sensitive information once they become comfortable with the mediator and the mediation environment. Many businesses opt for mediation to avoid adverse publicity, which may have an even larger negative impact upon the company than the dispute itself.
- *Foundation for later resolution.* Even when a dispute is not resolved in the formal mediation process, a foundation often is set for a later resolution either directly by the parties or with the mediator's continued involvement.

2.6 Why Some Mediations Fail

A failed mediation may be a result of the participants' lack of understanding of the process rather than any failure of the process itself. As an example, lawyer participants who are litigators and inexperienced with the mediation process simply may not be able to make a successful transition from a litigation to a mediation mindset.

The relatively unstructured nature of the mediation process makes certain lawyers uncomfortable. They are far more accustomed to litigation and the boundaries dictated by rules of evidence and procedure. Some lawyers do not understand, for example, that the client will be directly involved in the process or will be asked questions such as "what do you need the most" or "how do you feel" about the adverse party. While these questions may be completely unrelated to the merits of the claims and defenses in a lawsuit, they reveal perceptions and interests that affect the process and promote opportunities for resolution.

Lawyers also are nervous about voluntarily sharing "too much" information—even though if litigation did ensue, the discovery process would likely quickly lead to the production of the information held back.

Other lawyers believe, incorrectly, that there is no downside in a mediation since the process is non-binding and they do little preparation. As a result, significant opportunities to achieve client objectives often are lost by such counsel. A serious mediation requires investment: time, attention, and a willingness to share information and analysis with the other side.

Some mediations fail because of a communications failure, not between the parties or their representatives, but between a lawyer and his or her client. Some lawyers give their clients unrealistic expectations or simply neglect to advise their clients about the merits of their case on a regular basis. In these instances, clients are left without any realistic ability to assess the risks of litigation. Similarly, but equally importantly, lawyers may not prepare their clients adequately on the procedural costs of litigation (financial or in terms of time and focus lost) or overestimate the value of the ability to appeal an adverse decision in court. Litigators should be prepared to have a brutally honest discussion with their clients about the costs, disruption, and ultimate uncertainty of all litigation, regardless of how efficiently counsel runs the case (see chapter 6).

Additional reasons why some mediations are unsuccessful include:

- Maintaining a litigation mindset by focusing on the past and an assessment of who was right and wrong, attempting to win the mediation, holding back information for strategic advantage, refusing to acknowledge weaknesses, and failing to focus on forward-looking business solutions
- Absence of key decision maker or business executives in possession of important knowledge about the dispute and the effect of potential resolutions on the business
- Absence of necessary party
- Wrong client representative in the room
- Case not suitable for mediation
- Mediation occurs before parties have adequate information to make reasonable settlement evaluation and the mediation process is not used to fill information gaps—perhaps because clients are hesitant to invest sufficient time or money in the process
- Different and inflexible estimates of litigation risk
- Failure to identify or understand the other side's motivations, perspectives, and perceptions
- Hostilities so great that they prevent the parties from communicating effectively
- Lack of patience and perseverance

Finally, some mediations fail because the mediator is either unskilled or inappropriate for the case. In opting for mediation, selecting a *skilled* and *experienced* mediator is the single most important step a party can take to enhance the likelihood of a successful outcome; looking for expertise in the transactions or industry at issue may also be critical (see section 6.6).

2.7 Proposing Mediation to an Adversary

Once the business client has opted for mediation, counsel and the client should develop a specific proposal for mediation to present to other parties. Besides presenting the generic benefits of mediation, such as speed, cost savings, time savings, flexibility of the ultimate solution or remedy and privacy, counsel should outline specific benefits likely to serve the opposing party's particular needs.

Assessing the interests of other parties involved in the dispute will help counsel and the client determine whether those parties have an incentive to adjudicate or mediate. For example, the opposing party may desire a public forum, an interest that will not be served through mediation. Once counsel has assessed the other side's interests, counsel can present a customized proposal that demonstrates to the other side the benefits offered by mediation. Having a business executive make the proposal to their counterpart should also be considered.

Some lawyers are reluctant to propose mediation because of a concern that the suggestion will be interpreted as a sign of weakness. We emphasize that this concern should be far less than when making direct overtures to settle, and that indeed, a proposal to mediate can be made in such a manner as to convey a sign of strength. For example, counsel can suggest that the merits of the client's positions are so strong that any skilled mediator would no doubt validate this opinion.

Similarly, a proposal to mediate made by one business executive to another can be framed as an acknowledgement that both parties want to get back to business with the dispute behind them but after much back and forth need a fresh set of neutral eyes to help them step back and refresh on what brought them into the dispute in the first place.

If it is significantly in the client's interest to mediate, counsel should consider including specific incentives for the opposing side if they are reluctant to participate in the process. For example, the party proposing mediation might offer to pay for the initial mediation session. Counsel may also want to consider accepting as the mediator a candidate proposed by the other side so long as the mediator is competent, has the requisite expertise as necessary and no conflict exists. In fact, sophisticated plaintiff's attorneys often will consider accepting the defendant's candidate knowing that the defendant's choice will have more persuasive power in caucus.

Counsel and the client should also examine the corporate culture of the opposing party. If a party to a dispute has adopted a corporate policy favoring mediation, counsel can remind the party of this commitment made prior to the dispute. For example, counsel should determine whether an opposing party is a signatory to the CPR Institute Corporate Policy Statement on Alternatives to Litigation. More than 4,000 companies have committed to this pledge, which obliges subscribing companies to seriously explore negotiation, mediation, or other ADR processes in conflicts arising with other signatories before pursuing full-scale litigation. Additionally, many companies have entered into industry-wide "treaties" favoring alternative approaches in disputes between signatory companies.

Some private organizations or even mediators themselves are willing to help "convene" a mediation by making the proposal to opposing parties. A neutral person or organization may be in a better position to educate a reluctant party about the benefits of mediation. These organizations are also in a position to provide a range of related services, including the submission of mediator candidates and administration of the entire mediation process.

Finally, concerns about suggesting mediation and looking "weak" can, of course, be removed entirely by building a mediation step into a dispute resolution clause in a contract—or adopting a "mediation window" in an arbitration agreement or procedural order requiring the parties to mediate at a certain point in time during the life of the adjudicated process.

CHAPTER 3
THE TYPICAL STAGES OF BASIC IN-PERSON AND VIRTUAL COMMERCIAL MEDIATIONS

3.1 Introduction

Mediations vary in style, length, and rules of conduct. These variations have increased with both the legal and business community's experience with mediation generally over the past decades, the use of more flexible remote, virtual mediation options, and the consideration of business arrangements as part of a resolution.

While mediation has typically meant the day that the parties get together to talk with the help of a mediator—and staying late into the night until a resolution or impasse is reached—we are encouraging parties involved in commercial mediations to view mediation as a more nuanced process consisting of a number of steps over time that include preparation with the help of the mediator, in-person or remote live sessions, follow-up, and additional discussions until a resolution is reached or the parties and the mediator agree that further discussions are not likely to be productive.

In this chapter, however, we discuss the structure of a typical, basic business mediation, with significant attention in section 3.3 to the virtual environment. It is important for parties and counsel in a mediation to understand these patterns in order to maximize the potential for a successful result and assess whether variations will be helpful.

3.2 The Stages of a Basic Commercial Mediation

3.2.1 Preliminary Conference with Mediator—Establishing Ground Rules

After the parties select the mediator (see section 6.6), the mediator usually will start the process by convening a conference of all counsel by telephone (or increasingly, via a virtual platform such as Zoom) or in-person to selection a location(s), date(s), and time(s) for an in-person or virtual mediation session and to establish the ground rules for the mediation process. The mediator will then confer with counsel to get a basic understanding of the controversy and to determine what advance preparation is necessary. As the practice of mediation has developed over time, sophisticated practitioners have accepted the fact that significant preparation is important to the success of the overall mediation process. If a dispute is in litigation, the mediator will determine what pleadings, memoranda, written expert reports, underlying transactional documents, or other writings need to be reviewed in advance of the mediation. In this initial stage, the parties and the mediator will also determine the terms of engagement.

The mediator will discuss with the parties what written statements, if any, should be prepared specifically for the mediation, what oral presentations should be made, if any, at the mediation, and which representatives of the parties should participate in the mediation.

The following is a list of preliminary matters typically covered in the initial conference with a mediator:

- Ground rules and possible modifications; virtual mediations will require attention to technical details and many other issues uniquely related to the remote environment as discussed in section 3.3
- Each party's need for documents or information from the other party to close or narrow information gaps
- Submission of written statements and other documents to the mediator on a confidential basis
- Less commonly, but particularly recommended for matters that are not yet the subject of an adjudication process, whether an exchange of written statements between or among the parties will be helpful in clarifying positions on business or legal issues
- Appropriate representatives of the parties who will participate in the mediation process in some capacity and/or attend the mediation sessions, and the extent of their authority
- Identification of any non-party stakeholders who should also participate in and/or attend the mediation sessions
- Scheduling of any ex parte conferences prior to the mediation sessions
- Scheduling of dates, time, and location of mediation sessions
- Mediator's terms of engagement
- Allocation of mediation fees (especially in multiparty cases)

3.2.2 Deciding Who Should Attend Mediation In-Person or Virtual Sessions

Before the mediation sessions, the mediator usually will discuss with counsel which representatives of the parties should attend and whether it is necessary to have higher-level management representatives, insurance carriers, or others present at the mediation. Unless the key decisionmakers are present, the mediation process may not have its best chance for success. If the representatives require higher levels of authority for final approval of a settlement—what mediator Jeff Kichaven has called "the real decision-maker"—the mediator will discuss the need to have these persons available.

If the presence of additional persons is likely to advance the process, the mediator will encourage their participation in the mediation. For example, a mediator may encourage a businessperson who relies on an accountant for business advice to have the accountant present at the mediation.

Particularly in a large corporate setting, it may simply be impractical to expect that all stakeholders who need to have input into an agreed resolution will be able to be present at the mediation, even with the increased flexibility of remote mediation. In this case, the mediator will work to ensure that she understands who those individuals are and encourage each side to do its homework in discussing possible resolutions that will be acceptable to the business in advance of the live sessions, as well as having these individuals available as necessary to step into a live joint session as necessary. Inside counsel can play a critical role in connection with this diligence. (Having a virtual mediation, of course, increases the likelihood that key stakeholders can be involved in the joint discussion and is one of the advantages of that forum, as we highlight in section 3.3.)

With respect to issues such as participation, exchange of information, and other matters relating to the structure of the mediation, the parties may decide these questions in advance of selecting a mediator in a manner best suited to the controversy. Flexibility in the design of the process is one of the key advantages of mediation. The parties should also recognize that the mediator may have additional insights about structure that will enhance the likelihood of a successful mediation.

3.2.3 Exchange of Information

One of the goals of mediation is to avoid costly and time-consuming discovery, while recognizing that the parties may need additional information to assess their positions and possible outcomes. Since mediations often are held without any agreements on discovery, it may be necessary for the parties to exchange certain materials and documents as a preliminary step to an effective negotiation. For example, a plaintiff will invariably be encouraged to submit to a defendant, in advance of the mediation, a statement supporting its claim for damages. The mediator, therefore, usually will ask the parties whether they need to exchange information or documents in recognition of the fact that gaps in information may cause the mediation to fail.

The mediator may encourage this type of information exchange by pointing out that in a litigation or arbitration, the exchanges will need to occur anyway. We also encourage parties to view this robust process as good preparation for any adjudication and a way to avoid nasty surprises. The mediator will work to ensure to the extent possible that the information exchange feels reciprocal to both sides—in other words, both sides are "showing their hand" to the same or similar extent.

3.2.4 Pre-Mediation Written Submissions and Conferences

While pre-mediation submissions are required in most mediations, the contents of these submissions vary greatly. As noted, some mediators may require the parties to exchange submissions, especially if the mediation occurs early in the life of a dispute and the parties need to learn more about each other's legal positions.

Either in addition to any exchanged submissions or as the only required submission, most mediators will require a confidential ("eyes only") submission. In this confidential submission, in addition to a discussion of the parties' respective legal positions and their perceptions of their strengths and weaknesses, the mediator will ask the parties to discuss the history of any settlement negotiations, any underlying problems in the dispute, any barriers to settlement, any personality issues that need to be considered, corporate policy issues that may be relevant, views concerning underlying interests, and suggestions for creative paths to resolve the dispute.

In substantial or complex disputes, many mediators will hold *ex parte* meetings with counsel and, in some instances, with the parties, in advance of the mediation. In these meetings, the mediator will learn more about the business operations of the parties, obtain necessary confidential information, develop a better understanding of the parties' rights and interests, begin the process of building trust, and develop a structure for the mediation best suited to the particular dispute.

3.2.5 Initial Joint Session

Most initial mediation sessions begin with a *joint session*—representatives of the parties and their counsel assemble together with the mediator in the same room. The session will open with the mediator's introductory remarks, which typically will include the following:

- An explanation of the process
- An explanation of the mediator's role in the process
- A statement confirming the mediator's neutrality
- A statement summarizing the mediator's preparation in advance of the proceeding
- A full explanation of the confidential nature of the proceeding
- Additional guidance from the mediator regarding how to approach the discussions in order to have the greatest possible chances of success
- A statement seeking a commitment from the parties to make a good-faith effort to resolve the dispute

Many counsel equate the concept of a joint session with an opportunity to make an opening statement or presentation about their case. These concepts need to be distinguished. We would never begin any business mediation without some form of joint session with the mediator. Whether or not, after the mediator's remarks, it is a good idea for counsel to make what has been referred to as an opening statement is an entirely different question, and in some parts of the country, a joint session in this sense of the word is disappearing for the reasons we describe below.

An advocate's opening statement potentially can serve a number of purposes. First, it permits each party to argue the strengths of its own position and the weaknesses of positions taken by opposing parties on business issues, the facts, and legal claims. Second, it affords each party the opportunity to present its case directly to the key decision maker within the adverse party's organization. As a consequence, each party hears the other side's arguments unfiltered by its own counsel. Third, it gives the client representatives an opportunity to tell their story to the other side, as well as an opportunity for their "day in court" before moving on to the business of settlement. Fourth, it permits the mediator to be educated further on the issues and to seek clarification by asking follow-up questions.

Given the potentially volatile nature of the process, however, the mediator usually will exercise a high degree of control at the beginning of the initial joint session. Parties will be permitted, even encouraged, to express their feelings, but they will not be permitted to be overly argumentative. The mediator will prevent the initial session from getting out of control and will intercede if the parties become intransigent or threaten to abandon the mediation process.

If opening statements are made, at the conclusion of these initial lawyer presentations in a joint session, many mediators will ask questions for the purpose of clarifying facts or legal positions. In some instances, a mediator will ask questions (knowing the answers in advance) solely to permit one of the disputants to gain a better understanding of its adversary's positions or perspectives.

On the other hand, over time, many experienced counsel and mediators have come to the conclusion that the risk that such opening statements will get the initial mediation session off to a very bad start by inflaming the situation is not worth the benefit, especially when there are substitutes that may achieve the laudable goals of an opening statement without the risks.

Whether or not to have opening statements is not a one-size-fits-all assessment and should be discussed with the mediator. The "disappearing joint session" phenomenon often discussed in the field (being particularly acute on the West Coast of the United States) is in part a result of more experience with the process over the years and recognition of the importance of preparation, discussed further below.

A key question is to ask whether or not an exchange of position papers (rather than the more traditional confidential mediation statements) can serve most or all of the beneficial purposes of live opening statements while ameliorating the potential problems. We think such exchanges can indeed be very helpful and should be carefully considered as a reasonable substitute for opening statements in business cases. In a personal injury case, plaintiffs' attorneys often will want to "shock and awe" the defense with pictures of injuries and give the defense a robust preview of how their case will come across to a jury in an impressive opening. This type of advocacy is not usually necessary—or even advisable—in a business case.

Another question is whether or not, even without a full-blown lawyer opening statement, to have the business people say a few words about what might have gone wrong and how they hope to resolve the matter in a business-oriented way. This is always worth considering as long as the words are sincere and the business executive refrains from arguing the merits of the case in place of her attorney. A cautionary note: the business representatives should appreciate that appearing to "cheat" on agreed ground rules by straying into the merits can be and will be even worse than an ill-advised opening statement by an attorney.

3.2.6 Initial Caucus Session

Typically, the mediator will separate the parties and meet with them privately at the conclusion of the initial joint conference. In some cases, however, depending on the mediator's own style, and especially where the parties in a joint session are engaging in meaningful and constructive dialogue, the mediator will not separate the parties (at least initially).

Separate *caucus* sessions permit the mediator to identify and explore underlying interests and business goals and to clarify each party's perspectives. In these sessions, the mediator will encourage the parties to speak more openly and to disclose confidential information in order to identify barriers to settlement and to assist parties in overcoming these barriers (see section 5.2). The mediator will remind the parties of the mediator's obligation to not disclose confidential information. If the mediator believes that disclosure of confidential information will help advance a party's interests, the mediator will seek express authorization to communicate this information to the other side before making any such disclosure.

In most commercial disputes, mediators will move relatively quickly into separate sessions. Typically, parties will feel the need to argue the merits of their positions further at the outset of the initial caucus session. Rarely will the parties open up to a mediator quickly. Instead, they often will try to convince the mediator of the correctness of their positions in an effort to have him or her serve as an advocate in the negotiations (see section 4.5).

The mediator invariably will anticipate the parties' need to reargue their positions. Given the need to build trust, the mediator will take time to listen to these arguments and will remind the parties that the mediator must remain impartial in order to assist the parties in resolving the dispute. The mediator's patience and articulated confidence in the process is key to a successful mediation.

The mediator will use the early phase of the initial caucus sessions to establish a rapport with the parties, to earn the trust of the parties, to identify the negotiating styles of the attorneys and the identity of the real decision makers, and to ensure that she understands the parties' positions on disputed factual and legal issues. Eventually, she will begin to try to shift the parties away from their initial positions. In time, the mediator will try to move the parties away from finger pointing and assessing blame to a focus on interests and a problem-solving approach to the dispute.

If, as often is the case, attorneys take the lead in the joint session, the mediator in the caucus session will involve the party representatives by posing questions directly to them. It is not uncommon for a mediator to direct questions to representatives of the parties such as: "How do you assess your own case?" "What are your weaknesses?" "How do you feel about this dispute?" "What do you really want?" "What do you really need?" "What do you need the most?" "What do you think the other side really wants?" These questions permit the mediator to assess the parties' real needs and open the door to possible solutions.

Mediators will pay careful attention to when it is appropriate to begin discussing concrete numbers or offers more generally. In general, the initial caucus will not be the right time, despite potential impatience to "get to the point" evinced by lawyers and/or their clients, because the parties have not adequately considered their risks and business options. Numbers are based upon risk analysis and the desire for a business solution; these subjects need to be explored substantively beforehand.

3.2.7 Subsequent Joint and Caucus Sessions

After the initial caucus sessions, the hard work of negotiation begins—moving the parties to the common ground of mutual agreement. Typically, the mediator will not issue evaluations or opinions during this process (see section 4.4). Rather, the mediator will employ a number of techniques designed to test the limitations of the positions previously taken by the parties (see section 4.6).

In follow-up caucus sessions, however, the mediator is likely to play devil's advocate—testing the validity of positions without revealing his or her own views. The mediator will encourage the parties to consider their risks and costs if the dispute is not resolved at the mediation stage and to assess their alternatives to any proposed negotiated resolution. The mediator will also make an effort to move the parties away from positional bargaining over the strengths and weaknesses of the so-called merits and toward the underlying business interests.

Using shuttle diplomacy, the mediator will brainstorm with the parties to identify settlement possibilities and will move between the parties, carrying perspectives and suggesting settlement proposals. In our more complex cases, we often ask the parties to write down their proposals—which often have multiple parts beyond money—to ensure team agreement and accuracy, and to consider having the parties present the proposals to each other in order to generate a dialogue and give the receiving side a chance to ask questions. This is the most sensitive stage of the communication process.

It is imperative that a mediator not communicate to the other side a party's position on settlement without an express understanding that he or she is released to do so. Any breach of this commitment may well lead to a breakdown of the entire proceedings.

In some mediations, the mediator will continue to move between the parties in caucus sessions and will not suggest any further joint session until the end of the process.

In other mediations, a return to joint sessions may prove to be helpful, especially when it is necessary to clarify information or where the parties are making an effort to restructure a business relationship. These joint sessions often are suggested by the mediator and may not include all participants. Joint sessions that are limited to business participants, for example, can get the discussions back to a business negotiation from a more adversarial approach.

3.2.8 Agreement

When a mediation is successful and the parties reach a settlement—an event that may happen at any point in the process—the mediator will generally insist that the parties execute a written settlement memorandum or term sheet, or at the very least, craft an email to be distributed amongst the participants outlining the agreed terms.

Placing an agreement in writing will reveal whether there is a true "meeting of the minds." Often, a final and comprehensive settlement agreement will follow, one that incorporates all of the terms, including general releases from liability or additional business terms that have been negotiated that change the deal. If an arbitration or litigation is pending, parties will agree to terminate the action and may also request that the arbitrator or court enter a judgment based on the settlement agreement. The failure to execute a written agreement may well undo all the hard work and may threaten the successful conclusion of the mediation. In the absence of a written agreement, the parties may leave the mediation with differing views as to terms of an agreement or may later have remorse about its terms.

Many mediators discourage the drafting of a full and comprehensive agreement as part of the mediation process. (And, since their role is not to give legal advice, they generally will not draft such an agreement, although they may be willing to provide comments in the interests of avoiding future disputes.) Rather, where such an agreement is necessary, they will encourage the parties to draft the agreement at a later time in order to avoid the potential for a settlement to break down over the drafting process itself. Before closing the proceeding, the mediator will secure agreement from the parties about the drafting and execution of a more comprehensive settlement document. Typically, mediators will offer their continuing assistance with any future problems the parties cannot resolve on their own.

When seeking to draft an enforceable mediated settlement agreement, parties and their counsel should focus on "Contract 101" principles such as setting forth the material terms of the agreement and avoiding circumstances that might constitute a defense to enforceability under traditional contract law principles, such as duress or lack of authority. The fact is, however, that with knowledgeable counsel involved, mediated settlement agreements have generally survived challenge in court by the "remorseful buyer."[10]

3.2.9 Possible Recess, Adjournment, and Termination

A mediator will consider a recess for a short period of time in situations where, for example, the parties are not prepared, the parties need more time to reflect upon their settlement positions, or additional time is required for higher levels of authorization.

A mediator may adjourn a mediation indefinitely when he or she believes the parties have reached an impasse not likely to be overcome at the mediation session. Recognizing that parties often reassess their positions after a mediation session, the mediator will usually offer to remain available either by telephone or in person for future mediation sessions. Persistence, as well as patience, are hallmarks of a good mediator.

A mediator may determine that an amicable resolution is virtually impossible because there are irreconcilable differences or because one of the parties is unwilling to participate in the manner required. In such a case, the mediator is likely to advise the parties of the problem and terminate the mediation proceeding. However, an experienced mediator will not make such a decision quickly in recognition of the likelihood that obstacles to settlement can be overcome by skillful and patient probing and working through what often appears to the parties to be a hopeless stage in the process.

10. *See* Edna Sussman and Conna A. Weiner, *Striving for a 'Bulletproof' Mediation Settlement Agreement*, 33 Alt High Cost Litig 49 (2015), https://onlinelibrary.wiley.com/doi/10.1002/alt.21575.

3.3 Virtual Mediation—Assessment and Best Practices

Before the COVID-19 pandemic, many of the preparation steps outlined in this book took place over the telephone and via email. The stages of a typical and more complex mediation session also, however, can and have been successfully implemented over virtual platforms, with much learning and progress telescoped into a very short period as a result of the pandemic. As of this writing, the most commonly used platform is Zoom, with its flexible main session and breakout room technology substituting for joint sessions and private caucuses. (Other types of fully non-video online dispute resolution processes, particularly in courts and for e-commerce, continue to develop, with important questions relating to artificial intelligence, smart contracts, blockchain, and other sophisticated technologies. We focus here on "virtual" mediation.)

Fully remote, virtual mediation is here to stay, with some of our in-house counsel business contacts stating that they will now assume they will proceed with mediations virtually and have to justify for strategic reasons the additional cost and inconvenience of proceeding in-person. Simply put, whether or not to proceed virtually or in-person—or using some hybrid process combining virtual and in-person sessions—must now be part of the standard list of preparation questions for counsel and business representatives.

It is absolutely critical, however, to prepare even more extensively for a virtual mediation than an in-person mediation to make sure that some of the disadvantages of the technology and lack of in-person contact are ameliorated. Virtual processes are less amenable to improvisation and last-minute strategizing or document sharing, and technical glitches can be extremely disruptive. It is also important to take steps to ensure fairness and transparency.

As economist Thomas Sowell of Stanford University has wisely said in another context, "There are no perfect solutions, only trade-offs." On balance, however, most experienced mediators have discovered that virtual mediations replicate the in-person mediation experience remarkably well, and in many ways enhance it.

3.3.1 *The Advantages of Fully Remote, Virtual Business Mediations*

- Tremendous logistical advantages in terms of time and cost savings.
- These logistical advantages permit more stakeholders to attend the mediation itself, thereby potentially increasing the possibility of

settlement by having the right people on hand and making the discussion feel like more of a business negotiation rather than a process led only by lawyers. For example, key business people such as a chief financial officer, or the head of the manufacturing department involved in a dispute, may be able to attend all or part of a virtual mediation when time and cost would have prevented their attendance at an in-person session.

- The fact that each person has his or her own computer "square" (in Zoom)—rather than lawyers sitting at the head of a table—increases the feeling that all participants are equal and involved in problem solving.
- Participants may be more relaxed in the relatively informal setting of a video call and less likely to overreact.
- Tremendous flexibility in efficiently assembling different groups—beyond the "plaintiff" and "defendant" room—to work on various aspects of a potential settlement using the breakout room function and for the mediator to circulate quickly among these groups. This has enhanced the use of advanced techniques.

3.3.2 Key User Concerns Regarding Virtual Mediation

- Security/confidentiality.
- Technical failures.
- Lack of investment in travel to the mediation site and blocking off the time to be physically present makes the participants less committed to the process and therefore settlement less likely.
- Potential reduction in advocate effectiveness (lack of personal contact and ability to read body language, harder to communicate with client; less ability to apply pressure via video, shock and awe).
- Potential reduction in mediator effectiveness (lack of personal contact, harder to read body language, less able to apply pressure via video).
- Less engagement by participants, in part as a result of "Zoom fatigue" and ability to focus on emails and other distractions in their remote environment.
- No drop-dead end time reduces overall pressure to reach an agreement and increases the length of the session unnecessarily.
- Different time zones create disadvantages for those participants whose evening is approaching.

3.3.3 Best Practices to Enhance the Advantages and Ameliorate Disadvantages of Fully Virtual Mediations

1. **Security and confidentiality:** In general, the dispute resolution community has become comfortable with the security aspects of the Zoom platform, particularly since Zoom has made changes to reflect user concern, including with respect to the confidentiality of break-out rooms, so long as certain protocols are followed:
   a. Authorized participants must be clearly identified to the Zoom host and only authorized participants should be given the virtual link to the meeting. Passwords should be required. The "waiting room" feature must be engaged so that each participant is admitted to the main session. Any participants calling in by phone only should identify themselves immediately. The session should not be recorded, within Zoom or by anyone. No photos should be permitted on the screen (for example, of an exhibit) unless all agree.
   b. Participants must be reminded that the mediation is confidential. If they are participating from a home environment, they should try to find a room by themselves to avoid distractions and ensure that they cannot be overheard.
   c. Each participant should be visible to all other participants during joint sessions. Unless there is a break, all participants should keep their videos on—and all participants should be announced and authorized. In a home environment, in particular, it is tempting to have a spouse or relative informally consulting without anyone but that particular participant realizing that they are involved.
   d. The mediator should have a way to contact the inhabitants of a breakout room to announce that they are coming in to avoid overhearing attorney-client communications. This could be through texts, a cell phone call, a "broadcast" message to all participants that the mediator is now going to one of the rooms, or a simple announcement upon entering the room.
2. **Technology: adequate internet connectivity, lighting, sound, and backup communications—and practice:** Lawyers should ensure that they and their clients have adequate internet connectivity (best connections are hardwired through a direct ethernet connection rather than wireless; competing users at home should be asked not to download a movie during the session), visual (adequate camera positioning for a head on view of each participant and sufficient lighting via a ring light or other

device), and sound (need a headset or a better microphone?). In general, the rule should be "one person, one screen" (or laptop) rather than having participants on one side grouped together in front of one camera in a conference room. All this should be tested well before the mediation.

In addition, it is critical to have a way to communicate outside the Zoom environment via text or cell phone so that parties can talk to each other if technology fails, or they need access to counsel. And giving up when the technology simply isn't working well is more advisable than pushing ahead, especially when reconvening is relatively easy compared to an in-person session.

Finally, clients and lawyers should practice mediation sessions in a Zoom environment and ensure they feel comfortable with moving in and out of breakout rooms, have a game plan for communication, etc.

3. **Substantive preparation:** Using all of the techniques we recommend for early mediation (see section 3.3.3) are important to consider in a virtual setting. Exchanged and confidential written statements, exchanged key documents, and drafting potential settlement language ahead of time are critical to maximizing the time in a virtual session.
4. **Establishing interpersonal connections:** Preparation sessions should be more frequent and performed on Zoom so that the parties and the mediator get to know each other, and during the mediation participants should be required to keep their video on their screen turned on unless there is an agreed break.
5. **Who can speak with whom and when:** In a virtual environment, it is easier for a mediator to go back and forth among parties or assemble smaller groups than it is in an in-person environment. In fact, it can happen in an instant. This can be a tremendous advantage. However, having an understanding about who the mediator will speak with and when, and giving the mediator flexibility to make decisions, is important to discuss in advance with the mediator and participants, particularly clients. In addition, users should make sure that they have as many break out rooms set up by the mediator as they think they will need—one side's lawyers and clients, outside counsel only, inside counsel only, businesspeople—to make it easier to have a side bar if they would like.
6. **Maintaining engagement/time zones:** Frequent breaks are important to ensure that "Zoom fatigue" does not lesson participant engagement. Parties should consider conducting a number of sessions rather than one lengthy Zoom session. The mediator will want to check in with

different groups in their breakout rooms more often or at least communicate with them via the "broadcast" function so that not too much time goes by without hearing from the mediator. And dealing with participants in different time zones will mean shortening sessions to ensure fairness.

7. **Time and pressure:** With enough preparation and agreed structure about the mediation sessions, a skilled mediator can create a sense of urgency and highlight the need for movement and progress. In addition, however, the ability to get back together as necessary can create a more productive environment for agreement, so long as clear next steps are delineated that will advance the discussions.
8. **Documents and finalizing agreements:** Handling documents is one of the more difficult challenges in a virtual environment, but these issues are manageable with certain protocols depending on the complexity of the case. Screen-sharing on Zoom or similar platforms can reduce communication among the participants as their video screens are reduced. One solution is to share hard copies of key documents ahead of time so that everyone has access to them "off screen." During the mediation, documents can be shared by email. Term sheets and settlement agreements can be shared by email or on the screen; electronic signature technology can be used to sign documents (such as signed PDFs or DocuSign) Many mediators and attorneys are moving to multiple screen environments that permit users to look at people on one screen and documents on another. As the use of a virtual environment becomes the norm, this next step investment in multi-screen technology may be important.

3.3.4 Hybrid Processes

The considerations above have assumed a fully remote, virtual mediation process. With the easing of pandemic restrictions and a return to the possibility of in-person sessions, inevitable questions will arise about the effectiveness of a hybrid process involving both virtual and in-person participants simultaneously, or in-person sessions followed by video follow up.

In our experience, we have found that, in an ideal world, all key participants should be involved in at least the initial sessions using the same modality: all Zoom, or all in-person. Inevitably, a participant participating over video when all others are participating in-person is disadvantaged, although video is certainly better than participation by telephone only. One person participating by phone only when others are in-person was always undesirable even before the pandemic. If the participant is not the centerpiece of the discussion but brought in only for a discrete role, this concern about hybrid participation is diminished.

Using video for preparation calls with the mediator and for follow-up sessions after an in-person session is a very effective way to ensure a robust and effective process.

In addition, we believe that the availability of video participation may likely increase pressure to involve remote decision makers live via video rather than through a late-night telephone call. This too will increase the robustness of the process.

As parties' experience with mixed mode and fully virtual mediations develop, there will be many additional, nuanced strategic considerations to explore to customize the process for success given the contours of a specific dispute.

On balance, however, as we have previously noted, most mediators have found that they can do their jobs effectively and that in many respects the mediation process can be greatly enhanced through virtual mediation of business cases.

Chapter 4
The Role of the Mediator

4.1 Introduction

A mediation advocate and her client who understand the perspectives and techniques of the mediator will be in a better position to develop a negotiating strategy designed to accomplish the client's objectives.

It is the presence of an impartial third-party facilitator, the mediator, that distinguishes mediation from traditional negotiation. The mediator's fundamental role is to facilitate communication and compromise among the parties and to help the parties reach an agreement. The mediator neither makes decisions nor judges the fairness of the outcome. Parties decide what is fair, what is not fair, what is acceptable, and what is not acceptable. Thus, it is the parties who are empowered in the mediation process, not the mediator.

Nevertheless, in complex commercial mediations, increasingly mediators are asked to evaluate each parties' positions and bluntly share their perspective or be evaluative. Some lawyers even transparently ask the mediator to "bang heads" to help the lawyers and their clients get past impasse and reach an agreement. Parties should assess whether or not this is appropriate in any given dispute and what expertise is required for this type of approach.

4.2 Qualities of an Effective Mediator

It is essential that all parties perceive the mediator as a totally impartial facilitator dedicated to working with the parties in an even-handed manner before any evaluative approach is attempted. An effective mediator should have as many of the following qualities as possible:

- Absolute impartiality
- Trustworthiness
- Mediation experience
- Good listening skills
- Ability to understand the law and facts
- Good people skills
- Good leadership and management skills
- Problem-solving skills
- Strong negotiating skills
- Flexibility
- Good business sense
- Patience
- A sense of humor
- In some cases, and depending on the result desired by the parties, expertise in a particular area of law, in negotiating transactions, or in a particular industry

While all of the above factors are important, it is imperative that a mediator be absolutely impartial, possess strong negotiating skills, and have the training and experience to understand the challenges presented by the mediation process. In selecting a mediator, parties also should consider the advantages or disadvantages of substantive expertise, use of facilitative and evaluative styles, and experience as a former judge (see section 6.6).

4.3 Importance of Credibility and Trust

For a mediation to have its best chance of success, the mediator must be trustworthy and credible. A mediator can earn the trust of the parties by showing complete impartiality and by actively listening to and reflecting back each party's positions and perspectives. Skilled mediators understand the importance of patience and the need for preparation, professionalism, and empathy for the parties' respective positions.

In many complex commercial mediations, it may also be important for the mediator to have general business, transactional, technological, or industry expertise in order to be able to discuss with the parties what is expected or what is "market" in a particular business arrangement, or suggest alternatives for restructurings of business arrangements that have not worked out.

Once a mediator has earned the parties' trust and confidence, the parties to a dispute are likely to be far more open with the mediator and to be more receptive to suggestions and proposals. Conversely, a breach of confidentiality or trust by a mediator will likely result in a failed mediation.

4.4 Mediator Styles and Approaches

Mediators have a variety of different styles and approaches. These styles and approaches often depend to significant extent on the mediator's career path before and after they began mediating—as a former or current litigator, former judge, current arbitrator or, less commonly in the profession, an industry expert (either a former in-house counsel or non-legal business executive) or transactional lawyer with direct experience negotiating business arrangements. Some mediators have had a combination of these roles and use these different "lenses" to help parties. (The role of mediator expertise is a recurring theme in this book.)

Generally, styles range from purely facilitative to strongly evaluative. However, there is an ongoing debate in the mediation community concerning the issue of style. Some mediators view mediation as primarily a facilitative process rather than an evaluative one. Some even view "evaluative mediation" as an oxymoron. Again, this can depend on the mediator's career path. However, effective mediators generally have flexibility and will use varying degrees of both styles. Moreover, in recent years, many mediators increasingly have recognized that a strong evaluative component is necessary in order to give the process its best chance of success; this is, in our experience, especially true in complex commercial mediations.

The issue of style is viewed by mediators in a number of different ways. Some see the dynamics of facilitative versus evaluative as much a matter of strategy or technique as a matter of style. Some mediators see style as a means of distinguishing between interest-based and rights-based approaches, active and passive approaches, or approaches determined by the mediator's personality. In addition, mediators with expertise in transactions or an industry will generally offer to parties the benefit of this expertise—for example, assessing parties' "commercially reasonable efforts" in the context of a particular transaction, discussing what is a reasonable business term, or the more likely interpretation of a contract provision—in driving toward a settlement, assuming that it was because they had this expertise that they were hired in the first place.

4.4.1 *Facilitative Style*

In using a purely facilitative style, a mediator will assist the parties in identifying and exploring interests, concerns, motivations, goals, common ground, and possible resolutions. However, the mediator will avoid drawing conclusions for the parties or offering opinions as to value, legal positions, rights, merits of the case, or potential litigation outcomes. In essence, the mediator will not evaluate the case. In facilitative mediation, the parties make all the decisions while the mediator encourages movement through probing and open-ended inquiries. In pure interest-based facilitative mediation, depending on the subject matter of the dispute, successful resolution does not require the mediator to possess technical or legal expertise. It is usually sufficient for an experienced mediator to be able to understand the dispute and the underlying interests of the parties.

Typically, a facilitative mediator will use caucus sessions to develop the parties' underlying concerns and interests. Spending time alone with the parties is usually necessary to fully explore underlying interests and positions and to identify potential solutions. Joint sessions often are reconvened when parties attempt to resolve a dispute by restructuring old agreements or entering into new ones.

4.4.2 *Evaluative Style*

While a facilitative approach was the most common approach in the early years of mediation, sophisticated corporate counsel and their attorneys today, especially in a commercial setting, have a preference for a mediator who can be more evaluative and challenge the other side's arguments and positions as well as their own.

Since decision makers and their counsel invariably have difficult making an objective assessment of the risks in litigation or arbitration, as we discuss in the section on cognitive barriers (the benchmark for making a sound settlement decision), it is by the use of evaluative techniques that a mediator can most effectively get parties to adjust the settlement expectations they established in advance of the mediation.

For this reason, it is not uncommon for counsel, when selecting a mediator, to include in a due diligence interview a question such as, "Are you an evaluative mediator?" Of course, a simple yes or no would not really be a meaningful response. We think of an evaluative approach as a continuum of techniques that get the decision maker to reassess unrealistic arguments or settlement expectations. At one end of the continuum, a mediator could raise an eyebrow or just say, "Really?" Moving along the continuum, a mediator could ask an advocate, "What are your strongest arguments, the ones you think will resonate in the other room?" Or, "Don't you have a problem with that argument?" Moving further along the continuum, a mediator could expressly challenge an argument by asking probing questions or by challenging specific positions. These questions or challenges often reflect the mediator's real views on important issues, but the practice falls short of a clear statement of the mediator's actual views. By reflecting on such questions, the participants have a greater opportunity to objectively evaluate the strengths and weaknesses of their own positions. Even more strongly evaluative, a mediator could ask the mediation advocate to assess the likelihood of winning an argument (on a percentage basis) or the likelihood of prevailing overall in court, and then suggest that the assessment is overly optimistic. At the other end of the continuum, a mediator could actually offer the parties her own evaluation of what might happen before an arbitrator or court.

When the participants in a mediation believe that an informed opinion is necessary, a mediator's technical, industry, or legal knowledge may help to move negotiations along. Under certain circumstances, a mediator's informed evaluation may assist in breaking an impasse or moving the process toward a final agreement.

A mediator may make an evaluation when interests are not the primary focus of the parties or when interest-based facilitative mediation is not successful. Since some evaluative mediations focus more on the merits of legal positions, the process may bear some resemblance to early neutral evaluation or non-binding arbitration. However, if the mediator is familiar with what market value is in connection with a type of transaction—or, put another way, what is commercially or technically reasonable or feasible in a particular business or industry setting—an evaluative approach may focus on the business interests and goals of the parties, not just on legal positions.

Typically, an evaluative mediator will use private caucus sessions to give a party the benefit of an evaluation without disturbing the equilibrium of the negotiations. When a party suggests an evaluation or opinion be given in a joint session to all parties, a mediator usually will seek the agreement of all parties before sharing such an evaluation or opinion.

When and whether to take an evaluative approach will be carefully considered by the mediator, although, as we have noted, such an approach is what sophisticated parties typically want. Without a cautious approach, a mediator risks a party believing that the mediator has taken the side of the adversary when they share even a devil's advocate opinion, Dwight Golann and Marjorie Corman Aaron suggest in their book *Mediating Legal Disputes*.[11] Certainly, an evaluative approach is most often reserved for later stages of the process. When evaluative mediation is being considered, the parties likely will consider whether the mediator is an expert in the subject matter or industry central to the dispute. If evaluative mediation is used, the parties may want the mediator to have knowledge of what they consider the real facts and all the applicable law. The mediator also will recognize that comments made in caucus sessions are received without an opportunity for cross-examination or rebuttal.

4.4.3 Combined Facilitative and Evaluative Styles—A Practical Approach

Given the issues involved in an immediate evaluative approach, most disputes require a combination of both facilitative and evaluative styles and approaches. In certain instances, alternating styles may be productive, and in fact, we believe that the styles should be viewed as a continuum, not either/or. For example, facilitation may be more effective in building trust and communication in the early stages of mediation, while evaluation may be useful in the later stages in an effort to break an impasse. Simply put, effective mediators must first ensure that they understand the position and perspectives of the parties—and demonstrate to the parties that they have done so before they begin developing an opinion. In commercial mediations, however, we have found that eventually, parties are looking for a significant dose of reality testing and questioning once they are satisfied that their positions and arguments are understood. Sophisticated advocates generally prepare their clients to expect to be challenged.

Modification of styles may be useful depending on the special circumstances of the case and the parties' needs, interests, or expectations. For example, a mediator may use a facilitative style to resolve all of the important issues and an evaluative style to assist in the disposition of minor issues.

When asking probing questions or challenging the positions of the participants (usually in caucus sessions), mediators often will mix facilitative

11. Dwight Golann & Marjorie Corman Aaron, Mediating Legal Disputes: Effective Strategies for Lawyers and Mediators (1996).

and evaluative styles. These questions or challenges often reflect the mediator's views on important issues, but, as we have suggested, the practice usually—but not always—falls short of a clear statement of the mediator's actual views. By reflecting on such questions, the participants have a greater opportunity to objectively evaluate the strengths and weaknesses of their own positions. Some mediators with expertise in an area will state their actual views but be careful to distinguish when they are conveying what the other side thinks or what a judge might think.

4.4.4 Narrow and Broad Approaches

Mediators taking a narrow approach are likely to focus on the legal positions taken by the parties. A mediator with a narrow approach will likely proceed with the kind of litigation-risk analysis more typically associated with a judicial settlement conference. In contrast, mediators taking a broad approach are likely to move beyond the legal positions taken by the parties to an exploration of the underlying interests. Additionally, a mediator with a broad approach will be more likely to have the parties view a dispute as a problem to be solved and, consequently, be more likely to have the parties work toward a business solution. Mediators with transactional or industry expertise are more likely to take a broad than a narrow approach and have more tools to assist the parties in generating and negotiating business options.

4.5 The Mediator As Negotiator

Most mediators perform the multiple roles of confidential listener (understanding a party's near–bottom line, but conveying that understanding only as a description of a gap, not an actual number), facilitator, evaluator, and negotiator. As a consequence, there are typically several negotiations proceeding simultaneously, including one between the adverse parties and another between the mediator and each of the parties and their counsel. Given the mediator's agenda, the negotiations between the mediator and the parties are usually more cooperative than adversarial.

While the mediator expects some level of cooperation, the parties and counsel often are restrained in their candor because of their need to posture with the mediator. Parties and counsel rarely convey their bottom line to the mediator at the outset of a mediation. Many mediators explicitly tell parties not to share their bottom line too early in the process because they do not want participants to box themselves in, and they know from experience that bottom lines change over time as a result of the mediation process. Marjorie Aaron has said that she will ask only for a party's next to final number. In time, parties usually become more open to a mediator who has earned their trust in recognition of the fact that partnering with the mediator may create the best opportunity to make progress with the other side.

4.6 Mediator Techniques and Strategies

To be fully prepared for a mediation, counsel and business participants should understand the techniques and strategies employed by the mediator during the mediation process. While some mediation techniques are similar to those employed by a judge in a settlement conference, many are specific to the mediation process. Some of the most frequently utilized techniques are discussed below. For mediators who adopt some of the extensive preparation techniques that we recommend in this book, these techniques also may be utilized during preparation meetings taking place prior to group mediation sessions.

Taking a step back, many mediator techniques involve encouraging parties to slow down, take a fresh look at their dispute, assess probabilities, focus on the future and their best next steps with better information, and not overreact to proposals they do not like.

4.6.1 Setting Expectations

A mediator will work hard to understand the parties' goals at the outset and may ask the parties for help in stating them. We have found, however, that an explicit statement of what is reasonable to expect from the mediation process can help prepare parties to accept less than their desired outcome in the interests of getting back to business and putting disputes behind them. For example, explicitly acknowledging that no one should expect to feel that they have "won" the mediation after the process is concluded, and that each side may feel unhappy about the numbers or the deal but will be better off overall can orient the process in the right direction from the start. Focusing on the trade-offs involved in resolving a dispute amicably and what is a better rather than a best outcome for each side is important for any settlement to succeed.

As lawyers have become more experienced with mediation over the past decades of practice, these messages will not come as a surprise, but they are worth repeating.

4.6.2 Information Gathering

Both before any live group sessions and in early live sessions, the mediator will attempt to gather as much information as possible concerning the parties and the dispute to ensure that she understands it and that the parties appreciate each other's perspectives. The mediator will ask open-ended, probing questions to get a sense of the issues and the positions of the parties. The mediator's initial objective will be to identify and explore all the possible elements associated with the contested business and legal claims, including the factual background, the overall business/industry context, legal issues, the elements of each cause of action, possible defenses, and evidence that supports such claims or defenses.

At this early stage, the mediator will explore the parties' need for settlement, any settlement offer currently on the table, the rationale behind a party's offer, how and why a specific offer was made, what signals such an offer may send to the other side, and why such an offer may be acceptable or unacceptable to the opposing party.

With the extensive preparation steps we recommend in this book, a significant amount of this type of background information gathering may have taken place before the live mediation sessions commence, either with the mediator, through exchanges of information between the parties, or both. This type of upfront investment saves tremendous time during the group sessions, and we have found that the amount of preparation is directly related to the likelihood of success in achieving settlement.

4.6.3 Minimizing Hostilities

Especially in caucus sessions, the mediator will allow the parties to express their feelings in an effort to defuse hostility. The mediator's goal is to give the parties a sense that someone is listening to their side, without damaging the potential for resolution. By using noninflammatory language and focusing the parties on the key issues, the mediator often can minimize existing hostility:

> Party A: "Those liars defrauded me."
>
> Mediator to Party B: "Although I know you think otherwise, Party A thinks that you did not tell them some things that were important for them to know in order to make the decision, and here's what those four things are and why they were important to them. What is your perspective?"

The reduction of hostility, often by breaking down reactions into more objectively stated component parts, may enable each party to better understand the perspective of its adversary and to make a more objective analysis of the dispute.

4.6.4 *Involving Client Directly*

By communicating directly with representatives of the parties, the mediator can overcome the posturing of counsel that typically occurs in a mediation. Parties usually will be more willing than their lawyers to depart from a discussion about legal rights in order to pursue a discussion about underlying business concerns and needs. In addition, the mediator often will develop and maintain communication between the parties in an effort to rebuild relationships and to move the parties toward agreement. (One litigator somewhat ruefully remarked to one of us that he had come to realize that, once claims and defenses were understood by his client and the other side, his job in a serious business mediation was to "get out of the way" and allow the businesspeople to talk to each other with the help of the mediator.) Inside and outside counsel should be prepared for this type of direct communication and understand that it is an important mediator settlement tool in business disputes.

4.6.5 *Prioritizing Client Concerns and Interests*

The mediator usually will help parties identify and rank their concerns, motivations, and needs in an attempt to understand fully the parties' underlying interests. During this inquiry, the mediator will direct the focus away from conclusionary positions and will assist the parties in prioritizing their interests and needs. To get to the underlying interests, the mediator may ask questions that are not fact-based, such as, "How do you feel about this?," "What is most important to you?," and "What is less important?" As the result of such probing, the mediator may uncover interests such as the need to remove an obstacle to a planned merger, the need to avoid being declared in breach of a bank covenant, an interest in avoiding a "hit" on the bottom line in a particular year (or quarter), an interest in avoiding publicity, or the desire for an apology. Interests such as these often are as compelling as—and sometimes more compelling than—an assessment of the risks and costs of litigation.

4.6.6 *Active Listening, Reframing, and Paraphrasing*

A skilled mediator will listen carefully to representatives of the parties, looking for as many signals as possible from their words and phrases. Words such as "important," "significant," and "substantial" often can convey a sense of the parties' positions on the issues and on possible resolutions. By paraphrasing or summarizing, the mediator can obtain a more complete understanding of the party's positions and avoid the possibility of error when expressing thoughts or positions to the other side. Also, the mediator's reframing an issue or paraphrasing helps to clarify for the speaker what he or she is asking. When paraphrasing, the mediator can express thoughts without using strong, emotional, or offensive language. By using these techniques, the mediator also is able to show empathy and enhance the level of trust.

4.6.7 Decreasing Commitments to Positions

By probing for underlying interests during the mediation process, the mediator can ease the parties toward interest-based negotiations. In so doing, the focus or commitment to legal rights and positions is relaxed and there is greater opportunity for open communication between the parties. As a result, negotiations become more flexible and new settlement options may be discovered.

4.6.8 Focusing on Potential to Preserve Business Relationships, Both Current and Future

The mediator will focus on the parties' business and strategic interests in reconciling their differences and attempting to reach a settlement. When the potential for a continuing relationship exists, the mediator will explore the advantages of an agreement based upon this relationship. Many disputes can be resolved by restructuring the terms of a relationship and by agreeing, for example, on issues such as price discounts, time extensions, adjustments in supply commitments, intellectual property cross-licensing agreements, or the expansion or limitation of territorial rights. Where parties have multiple relationships, some disputes can be resolved by restructuring the terms of a contract that is not the subject of the dispute.

Even without current relationships, sophisticated participants in an industry, particularly in a highly specialized technical field, like the life sciences, for example, will and should also focus on the likelihood of having to work with the other party again in the future to secure resources, supplies, software, or other expertise, or worry that having a reputation for suing a customer or business partner might be deleterious to their ability to conclude beneficial business arrangements in the future. Indeed, employees in one company may very well move to another company in the industry, bringing with them the memory of how a dispute was—or was not—successfully resolved.

4.6.9 Assessing When to Talk About Money or Begin Trading Offers—Anchoring

Skilled mediators will pay special attention to when it is appropriate to begin trading offers, particularly those including numbers, in the course of a mediation process. For example, parties often arrive at live sessions impatient to "get to the point" and complain that "we did not start talking numbers [discuss term sheets] until 2 in the afternoon." But numbers and more complex offers need to be based upon an analysis of positions and risk. Parties who "anchor" themselves too early at a high (or low) number (and therefore rely too heavily on this first move) may make the negotiations drag on inappropriately. As noted, slowing down the process to permit a more deliberative approach is part of the mediator's job.

Of course, the more investment in preparation the parties make the more quickly they can begin to work on concrete proposals.

Ultimately, this important timing question should be addressed with the mediator. As always, there is no one-size-fits-all answer. If significant preparation has been done, it may be appropriate for the parties to have exchanged numbers before conducting live, joint mediation sessions. It may be that one party will refuse to come to the mediation table at all without having some idea that the parties are within the same range—although a skilled mediator is likely to counsel that the fact that the parties are far apart is exactly why the mediation process is important and useful in the first place, and that without committing to the process, the parties can't assess what the end result may be.

4.6.10 Specific Techniques in "Pure Dollars" Disputes

In a pure dollars dispute, often referred to as a *distributive* dispute, the ultimate issue between the parties is the division of a sum of money represented by the difference between a demand and an offer. The mediator in such cases invariably will rely heavily on caucus sessions to identify each party's parameters and degree of flexibility. While the mediator will allow the parties to move slowly so that they may state their case, in an effort to build trust, the mediator will use all the probing techniques outlined in this chapter to find a way to bridge the gap.

The mediator often will ask the parties to provide a specific justification for their positions on the legal issues and value. However, when the parties are in substantial disagreement on particular issues, the mediator will move away from a discussion about positions to an exploration of the total dollar amount required to reach agreement. The parties are then free to provide their own rationale for any final settlement decision. One way to think about this transition is to view the start of the discussion over dollars as tied to a "principled" buildup to a number (for example, summing amounts tied to various alleged breaches and discounted by the likelihood of proving those breaches and the costs it will take to prove them to an arbitrator or judge), and then transitioning to pure "horse-trading" in order to get to an agreement.

Even in a distributive dispute, the mediator will look for possible creative options, such as the timing of payments or substituting other items of value for pure dollars.

Given the fact that the parties often are unprepared for the fact that a mediation can be a lengthy process, the mediator's principal challenges in orchestrating the negotiations will be to exercise patience, to exhibit optimism, and to do what is necessary to keep the parties from reacting in anger to a number that is not consistent with their assessment and instead keep talking. Focusing parties on the unavoidable fact that without movement—responding to an offer with a counteroffer—there can be no progress toward a settlement is critical to this exercise. Ultimately, the best antidote to a proposal that a party does not like ("That's insulting!") is to make a reasonable counteroffer and attempt to narrow the gap. As experienced mediators appreciate, the greatest motivation of the parties to settle is the perception that the case *can* settle; the greatest impediment to settlement is the perception that the case will not settle. For more on pure dollars disputes and negotiations over money and the motivation of parties seeking to settle, with specific, simultaneously hilarious and insightful examples of the cliches we have heard again and again in the context of these sorts of negotiations, we often turn to Little's book *Making Money Talk: How to Mediate Insured Claims and Other Monetary Disputes*.[12]

12. J. Anderson Little, Making Money Talk: How to Mediate Insured Claims and Other Monetary Disputes (2007).

4.6.11 *Reality Testing and Decision Analysis—The Sobering Concept of Cumulative Risk*

By testing the positions of the parties, the mediator will not only enable the parties to make a more objective risk analysis, but the mediator may also uncover a gap in understanding between the parties and their own counsel. By focusing on specific assessments, the mediator can move the parties toward a more realistic view of their cases and thereby greatly enhance the likelihood of settlement.

In caucus sessions, the mediator will ask parties to respond to an opponent's factual assertions, claim, or defense, or will demonstrate to the parties the weaknesses of their positions. In so doing, the mediator will explore weak points, consequences, and areas of overconfidence with respect to both the underlying business situation, liability, and damages. The mediator may ask questions that suggest that the facts or legal positions do not necessarily support the parties' conclusions. In addition, the mediator may remind the parties that the mediator is the only person in the room capable of making an objective assessment. Studies by leading programs on negotiation demonstrate that most parties and advocates tend to rely on the facts and law supporting their positions and give insufficient attention to the positions of the opposing party.

The mediator will ask the party to review the consequences of pursuing its position through litigation or arbitration. Any such discussion of the risks associated with litigation is likely to include costs, business disruption, loss of morale and productivity, burdens, discovery issues, timelines, possible appeals, jury uncertainties, judges' orientations, experts, witnesses' credibility, and collectability of any potential judgment.

Reality testing can be assisted in a numerical way that surprises many advocates and clients and helps them distance themselves from the emotions of their positions by looking at their chances based upon the cumulative risk of achieving their desired—or in some cases, very optimistically expected—outcome. At its simplest, and looking at it from the plaintiff's perspective (the analysis easily can be switched to the defendant's perspective as well), any potential payout needs to be multiplied by the probability of getting it, the full costs of achieving it, and the chances of collecting it. If, for example, the best-case scenario for a plaintiff is a $1,000,000 judgment and there is a 70 percent chance of achieving that number (and many attorneys will admit that this is aggressively optimistic, particularly in front of a jury), the risk-adjusted payoff must be discounted to $700,000. In other words, a rational actor would settle the case for $700,000 at least. If there are $150,000 in legal costs (attorneys' fees and expenses, including e-discovery, and many attorneys would admit this is a low number), the number goes down to $550,000. Add in a number reflecting the internal cost in terms of time and distraction, and that number goes down to $500,000. Finally, this amount will not be received for quite some time (for an arbitration, perhaps one year, and for a litigation two years or longer) and the judgment is at risk on appeal. The fully discounted, present value of that best-case scenario judgement goes down significantly even on the simplest, rosiest of assumptions. (And if there is a risk of collecting that money, and/or there may be costs expended to collect on a judgment, that also needs to be figured into the risk calculus, and it yet again reduces the number a rational actor would accept to settle the case.) Indeed, many mediation participants, when they focus merely on getting money today versus two years from now with the associated time and distraction, are convinced to modify their attachment to their principles.

Going a step further, a more nuanced approach, such as a detailed decision tree analysis—an analysis that can be supported by software programs designed for this purpose or by a simple Excel spreadsheet—can and should focus on the cumulative risk facing litigants at each step of a case, not merely on the overall chances of winning (for the plaintiff) or losing (from the defendant's perspective). A 90 percent chance of surviving a motion to dismiss, multiplied by a 70 percent chance of surviving a summary judgment motion, multiplied by a 65 percent chance of winning at trial takes the possible realized amount of a $1,000,000 judgment down very quickly. Many other steps can be added to the decision tree, with attendant probabilities, such as the chance of an expert being accepted by the court, etc.

Focusing on the uncomfortable math of cumulative risk can move parties away from their emotions and positions, slow down their thinking, and keep them on the path to an amicable resolution.

4.6.12 Applying Expertise to Challenge, Correct, or Modify Perceived Facts

Mediators with expertise in transactional, technical, and/or industry issues may, with the agreement of the parties, offer their views on material factual assertions. For example, a mediator with experience in pharmaceutical manufacturing contracts and associated regulatory requirements may offer views about the application of warranties to a particular set of facts in the context of a supply agreement or product acquisition. Similarly, mediators with industry expertise are well placed to discuss with the parties what it means to have made "commercially reasonable efforts" to achieve regulatory or commercialization milestones, including whether technical failure was an inevitable risk of a difficult project.

4.6.13 Overcoming Irrational Assessments

When testing whether parties have made realistic evaluations of risk and exposure, a skilled mediator will determine whether the parties' evaluations have been affected by irrational biases or *cognitive illusions*. The most common of these illusions are loss aversion, advocacy bias, certainty bias, hindsight bias, and reactive devaluation (see section 6.8.11). By sharing the conclusions reached by studies on cognitive illusions and biases (performed mostly in the past decade by graduate business schools and law schools), the mediator can help the parties overcome their irrational attachments to certain positions and make better settlement decisions. Many of the techniques outlined in this chapter are aimed at overcoming these cognitive illusions, including reality testing, for example. The mediator can be particularly helpful working with the parties to overcome loss aversion and reactive devaluation as set forth in the following sections.

4.6.14 Overcoming Loss Aversion

As discussed, loss aversion is a powerful cognitive force that may inappropriately weld parties to their initial benchmarks. Mediators will work to identify those benchmarks, test whether or not they are realistic, and change the options on the table to reduce the pain of perceived loss.

4.6.15 Proposing or Endorsing Solutions to Overcome Reactive Devaluation

The theory of reactive devaluation suggests that a proposal may be considered acceptable, satisfactory, or attractive when proposed by one's own side but suspicious, unacceptable, or unattractive when proposed by an adverse party. As Dwight Golann has commented, mediators are usually very reluctant to take outright ownership of a party's proposal. However, a mediator can help overcome reactive devaluation by offering one party's proposal to the other side as a hypothetical so that the proposal may be received more openly. In addition, the mediator may be able to endorse a party's proposal as made in good faith, a good next step, or worth discussing if a party has persuaded her that that this is true. Maintaining the trust and confidence of each side in the mediator's impartiality is critical, however, and whether or not to make such perceived endorsements must be carefully assessed.

Mediators with expertise in transactional structuring or an industry or other relevant experience may use these tools to come up with business solutions that are entirely their own and stated as such to avoid the harmful effects of reactive devaluation.

4.6.16 Identifying and Overcoming Barriers to Resolution

Parties to disputes frequently run into obstacles when they try to resolve disputes in direct and unassisted negotiations. A skilled mediator, especially in separate caucus sessions, can work with the parties to identify these obstacles and develop strategies for resolution. Chapter 5 discusses the common barriers to resolution and the techniques employed by the mediator to overcome them. These barriers are:

- Selective perception in making evaluations
- Wrong baselines
- Loss aversion (see section 4.6.14)
- Reactive devaluation (see section 4.6.15)
- Failure to communicate
- Gaps in information
- Insufficient focus on underlying interests
- Inability to align client's interests
- Disconnects between attorney and client
- Anger and embarrassment
- Behavior and tactics of parties and counsel
- Poor negotiating skills
- Inappropriate reliance on experts
- Preoccupation with winning
- Inability to break impasse (see section 4.6.15)
- Process barriers

4.6.17 Issuing a Formal Evaluative Opinion

Because of the potential perception of bias, mediators rarely offer unsolicited opinions of value, litigation outcome, or issue outcome without the agreement of the parties. Even solicited opinions are dangerous to the mediation process because of the potential for perceived bias. The mere appearance of bias can damage the integrity of the mediation process and impede or end progress. Such an opinion, however, may be appropriate if there is a deadlock in the negotiations.

4.6.18 "One Text" Approach to Reaching Agreement

In the "one text" approach, the parties or the mediator will draft a document of potential agreement, for example, a term sheet of potential business options. The mediator will then pass it back and forth or circulate it among the parties. As the text circulates and the parties' concerns surface, the parties or the mediator will revise the text to reflect the parties' concerns. Where there is some common ground and, especially in an effort to restructure a relationship, this approach may be a good tool for reaching agreement. However, this technique does not work well when the only issue is the payment of a sum of money.

In general, it is helpful to have one document that reflects the parties' offers back and forth, and it is especially useful to have the parties be the scribes to ensure internal agreement.

4.6.19 Impasse-Breaking Techniques

The skilled mediator will use a variety of techniques to break an initial impasse. Some methods include the basic tools of human psychology: the use of humor during a tense moment, the call for a recess, the creation of a new group dynamic by shifting the participants into different groups, and the reconvening of all participants into a joint session.

Other impasse-breaking techniques include:

- Proposing negotiating high–low bands or brackets within which negotiations will proceed
- Asking for linked concessions ("If they go up by X, will you come down by Y?")
- "Confidential listening"—attempting to understand the parties' real bottom lines after risk analysis and discussion—or "next to last number," as Marjorie Aaron has said—and then conveying a sense of that number or range verbally to the other side by way of guidance
- Refocusing on the importance of future relationships
- Reviewing the analysis of risk and cost

- Tracing the progress to date and acknowledging the possibility of an irreconcilable impasse so that the burden of breaking an impasse shifts to the parties themselves
- Asking the parties for their ideas
- Convening the top businesspeople—or even asking to speak to executives who have not participated in the mediation up to that point—and asking for their help (what expert mediator Eric Green has called the Napoleon Gambit)
- Requesting a "last best" offer
- Using a double-blind, "mediator's" proposal (see section 5.2.14). The mediator's proposal, when done after all else has failed, is delivered with the caveat that it does not reflect on either side's position but reflects only the mediator's perception of what the parties might accept—or in the cliché of the settlement world, what might make each side equally unhappy.

4.7 Mediator's Role at Conclusion

As we have noted, we advocate that mediation be approached as a process consisting of a number of steps, including preparation, live sessions (in-person or virtual), and follow-up.

As parties and counsel have gained experience with the mediation process over the years, it has become increasingly clear that a skilled mediator's job does not end at the conclusion of a live mediation session, particularly in connection with complex business disputes. After the formal mediation sessions, there are certain understandings that should be reached among the parties, whether or not settlement has been reached at the conclusion of the process.

If agreement is reached, the mediator should insist that the parties execute some form of a written settlement memorandum before the mediation session concludes, or at the very least, memorialize the terms in an emailed agreed term sheet. In some situations, the parties may also need a comprehensive written settlement agreement. In such an instance, the mediator will remain available to clarify misunderstandings and to help with unresolved issues and controversial provisions. The mediator also may offer to remain available to the parties to provide any other assistance that may be needed, including serving as a mediator or arbitrator of post-mediation disputes.

If agreement is not reached, the parties may want to address, either together or separately, the issue of the mediator's possible continuing efforts. Such involvement often can be a significant factor in producing a settlement.

In cases where a mediator has been retained in part because of their transactional and/or industry expertise, parties can consider having the mediator participate—perhaps as a silent observer or more actively—in the negotiation of a restructured or new business arrangement. The mediator may use this experience to offer suggestions on language, in joint sessions or privately, in order to avoid ambiguities that may result in future disputes.

CHAPTER 5
NEGOTIATION AND MEDIATION: OVERCOMING BARRIERS TO RESOLUTION

5.1 Introduction

Direct and unassisted negotiations can and should be considered as the initial path to resolving disputes. When successful, direct negotiation is the most flexible and cost-effective approach to resolving disputes whether or not litigation is pending—and business executives, along with their counsel, know their business needs and interests the best. The negotiation process, however, depends on the parties' ability to communicate, their willingness to make concessions, and their ability to recognize possible solutions. Especially in substantial commercial disputes, the barriers to resolution often are so significant that parties will not even attempt a negotiated resolution or often will reach impasse if they do attempt to negotiate. A skilled mediator often can overcome the many obstacles that prevent direct negotiation from succeeding. As discussed, the mediator's position as a neutral party who is new to the dispute can be the basis for inspiring a fresh look at difficult problems and overcoming some of the common barriers to resolution discussed in this chapter (see section 1.3).

5.2 The Common Barriers to Resolution

Below are the most common barriers to resolution in direct negotiations and an explanation of how a skilled and experienced mediator can overcome them. Many such mediators are generally aware of widely publicized research into how people make decisions and judgements and apply this in their thinking about helping parties to overcome barriers.

5.2.1 Selective Perception in Making Evaluations

Skilled mediators understand that, in many ways, they are fighting—and helping parties and their counsel fight—deeply rooted psychological tendencies that get in the way of the best decision-making and judgement.

Parties to a dispute and their counsel—both corporate counsel and outside counsel—invariably have difficulty making an objective evaluation of their own case. As we have found in our experience, and is widely understood in the field, self-interest and selective perception make it virtually impossible for any party or counsel to make a truly objective evaluation. Parties generally look for facts and law to support their own claims and overlook the evidence that might defeat their claims.

The familiarity of a party's own position exacerbates this effect. Research summarized well by Daniel Kahneman in his seminal book *Thinking, Fast and Slow* has also shown that repetition and familiarity significantly influence what people think of as true. Our more advanced, deliberate, and conscious mind (what Kahneman refers to as "System 2") is lazy and defaults often—too often—to the shortcuts of the more automatic "System 1," which relies on associations and intuition. One implication of this is that accepting a "fact" or legal position as true because it is familiar and therefore "safe," as a result of internal, defensive repetition by counsel and business executives, is cognitively easier than slowing down and thinking something through again—System 2 will take the easy way out if left to its own devices. Kahneman also identifies System 1 in general as a machine for "jumping to conclusions" and a contributor toward our tendency towards "confirmation bias"—along with System 2's tendency to search for confirmatory evidence. He notes the scientific evidence that participants in experiments presented with one-sided evidence are much more confident in their judgements than those presented with both sides.[13]

As a quote often attributed to Winston Churchill says, "Where you stand depends on where you sit." Simply because of the perfectly natural tendencies of the human mind itself, as consistently demonstrated by psychiatric and economic research over the years, a mediator may be the only person in the room who can make a truly objective evaluation and act as an agent of reality. While mediation is a facilitative process, especially in its beginning stages, mediators can appropriately challenge parties to consider whether their assessments are realistic without offering their own opinions on the merits. The "fresh look" and neutral position of a skilled mediator will help encourage the parties to slow down and rethink their oft-repeated, entrenched "truths."

5.2.2 Wrong Baselines—Loss Aversion

Parties in a negotiation commonly compare what is on the table with what they want or need or with what they consider to be fair. This establishes a baseline, and any "worse" or compromise result is experienced as a loss. This sets up a difficult psychological barrier to settlement, namely, the now well-accepted phenomenon of loss aversion. Economists and behavioral scientists have shown again and again that losses are extremely painful; in fact, people generally find losing to be twice as painful as an equivalent gain.

---

13. Daniel Kahneman, Thinking, Fast and Slow (2011). See generally chapters 2 and 3. This book is an outstanding contribution to the thinking about biases and heuristics in judgment and decision-making and well worth a careful read by mediators and parties.

Mediators will work hard to help parties step back and look at losses differently by determining what a party's benchmark is and encouraging them to reset or adjust them based upon a variety of factors. A skilled mediator can work with the parties to have them make a real-world comparison—one that compares what is on the table to the consequences that will occur in the absence of a negotiated resolution. A skilled mediator can challenge the parties to compare any offer with their *best alternative to a negotiated agreement* (BATNA) and their *worst alternative to a negotiated agreement* (WATNA). These become the baselines for what parties should accept or reject. Moreover, within these baselines, a skilled mediator will continually challenge parties to make realistic assessments.

Expanding the number of options on the table is also another useful way of resetting benchmarks. If a party is focusing on winning a seven figure judgment, terms that add value to a potential settlement other than mere money can move them away from that benchmark. In an oft-cited, perhaps apocryphal story, former Secretary of State Henry Kissinger ascribed his success in mediating agreements between Arabs and Israelis to the tactic of making the deal so complicated that no one could tell who was winning. Be that as it may, it can indeed be productive from a business perspective to look at different packages of options, which has the added benefit of reducing the strong psychological aversion to loss compared to previous internal benchmarks.

5.2.3 Reactive Devaluation

It is common for a party to reject a proposal made by an adversary if for no reason other than the fact that it was proposed by the adversary. Parties often are unable to assess the accuracy of information or accept a settlement proposal as made in good faith because they distrust the source. This phenomenon, like loss aversion—yet another psychologic heuristic—is known as *reactive devaluation* and is one of the most powerful problems in direct negotiation. Avoiding it is one of the great benefits of seeking the assistance of a third-party neutral. A skilled mediator can overcome reactive devaluation by presenting proposals as his or her own or by simply floating hypothetical proposals. After learning the disputants' general settlement parameters, a mediator often can float proposals likely to work for all parties.

5.2.4 Failure to Communicate

Once parties cross over into an adjudicated process such as arbitration or litigation, often, it is quite some time before there are any communications about settlement. Notwithstanding communications about pleadings, motions, discovery, and hearings, many litigators focus on trial preparation and strategy to the exclusion of settlement. Many lawyers avoid settlement initiatives to dispel any suggestion of weakness.

These tendencies are unfortunate, particularly in commercial cases. Settlement can occur—sometimes rather easily—if the parties communicate earlier and more openly. We have both acted as a mediator in a few cases where there were not only the usual gaps between the parties, but there were unrecognized overlaps.

In one case, a plaintiff stated that while it would accept $800,000 to settle its claim, the defendant would, in the plaintiff's view, pay only $500,000. The defendant confided that it would pay $900,000 to resolve the dispute, but it was certain the plaintiff would not settle for less than $1 million. Thus, there was an unrecognized $100,000 overlap. In this instance, both parties had made realistic assessments about value but inaccurate assessments about the other side's settlement position. A skilled mediator can facilitate good communication about settlement in cases where the parties are reluctant to do so on their own.

Ideally, the parties, particularly inside counsel, should strive to maintain an open line of communication about the possibilities of settlement throughout an arbitration or litigation. If direct communication is deemed too difficult, retaining a standby or standing neutral mediator or settlement counsel in advance of having an actual live mediation session is an advanced and efficient way to accomplish a parallel assessment and conversation.

5.2.5 Gaps in Information

Information gaps often present barriers to resolution. In preparing for mediation sessions, a skilled mediator will recognize the existence of such gaps and encourage the other side to provide information, such as a chronology of events in a contractual relationship, an accounting that supports a claim for damages, or case law that supports an important legal position. Information exchanges can help parties resolve disputes on their own. In one case involving a professional partnership dispute, the voluntary submission of an accounting resulted in the withdrawal of all claims and the termination of the dispute. In another, parties realized that one side had actually been paid much more than the presumptive plaintiff sought. Similarly, mediators are in a good position to clarify misunderstandings concerning the information provided or positions taken by either side. Mediators with expertise in a particular area of law, in transactions, or in a particular industry may be able to fill gaps based upon their own experience or help appreciate and identify gaps that need to be filled.

5.2.6 Insufficient Focus on Underlying Interests

Many parties engage in *distributive bargaining*, in which they exchange offers and demands in an effort to "divide the pie." As a consequence, these parties fail to capture an opportunity to create value. In contrast, a skilled mediator will encourage the parties to engage in *integrative bargaining* and take a more collaborative approach to negotiations. Parties are encouraged to focus on their interests as well as their rights and look for business-driven solutions. For example, distribution agreements can be restructured to provide for new provisions on territoriality or exclusivity. Supply agreements can be restructured to provide for future price discounts. If there is a continuing relationship, the parties will be asked to compare and contrast the issues in dispute with the importance of the relationship itself. Even in pure monetary disputes, parties can provide for creative means of monetary exchange. While much has been written about the potential for win-win in mediation, the possibility of such a result is not purely theoretical. We both have participated in mediations in which all parties have viewed a settlement to be *better* than their probable best result in litigation (taking into account the risks, costs, and distractions of litigation).

5.2.7 Inability to Align Client's Own Competing, Intramural Needs and Interests

Many parties and their inside and outside counsel perceive a dispute as having only one dimension—between the parties. In a typical dispute between two parties, the focus of negotiations will be primarily on differing views between the parties as to facts, claims, defenses, rights, obligations, experts, damages, issues of credibility, and outcomes. A more sophisticated analysis also will include the objectives, interests, and needs of each party separate and apart from their relationship to the other party, as the settlement barrier may have more to do with differences among and between the various constituent representatives of the client—particularly a large corporation—than differences between the parties. There is inevitably tension between the operating and central corporate functions (such as finance and tax) of a large corporation or between operating units, for example. In one mediation, the principal settlement obstacle was a disagreement about which division's profit-and-loss statement would be "hit" by a substantial payment to the plaintiff. In another, the principal obstacle was a disagreement about when to settle, given the fact that a settlement would require the company to restate its earnings. A skilled mediator will attempt to identify and recognize such problems and be in a position to conduct an intramural mediation between the client's representatives so that they can be aligned on settlement goals and positions. Do not be surprised if your skilled mediator asks for the latest organizational chart of the companies involved in the dispute.

5.2.8 Disconnects Between Attorney and Client

A one-dimensional approach to a dispute—focusing solely on differences between the parties—also ignores the fact that differences between an attorney and the client can create barriers to resolution. In many mediations, parties are unprepared to make realistic assessments because counsel has overstated the likelihood of success at the outset of a dispute or failed to communicate with the client on an adequate basis. Conversely, counsel may make a fairly reasonable litigation-risk assessment, only to have the client refuse to accept bad news. In a recent dispute, upon hearing the opinion of counsel, the president of a fairly large company stated to his own attorney, "I thought you were *my* lawyer."

In another dispute, at the conclusion of a successful mediation, an attorney privately said, "Thank you for telling my client what I could not say to him." Contingent fees also may present barriers to resolution. In one such dispute, counsel for the plaintiffs argued against a settlement the client was otherwise prepared to accept because the settlement would not produce a sufficient return on counsel's investment of time. Mediators are in a good position to discern and deal with any disconnect between attorney and client.

5.2.9 Anger and Embarrassment

It is not uncommon for business representatives to become angry or hostile to their counterparts in a failed business transaction or venture. Similarly, long-term partners and family members often stop speaking to one another as the result of differences of opinion in running the business. This hostility often prevents the parties from being able to jointly negotiate a resolution. A skilled mediator can provide a forum in which to facilitate communication and permit the parties to vent, overcome anger, and recognize the need for closure. In "angry" disputes, an apology can serve as a linchpin for resolution and, in some cases, a predicate for a rehabilitated relationship. Parties also can become entrenched in their settlement positions, especially when they draw a line in the sand in negotiations at an early stage of a dispute. Many parties, even in the face of new information, become too embarrassed to change their positions. A skilled mediator can, if it is not too late, intervene to prevent parties from drawing the line in the sand, or present new information and facilitate negotiations in ways that enable parties to change their positions and save face.

5.2.10 Behavior and Tactics of Parties and Counsel

In direct negotiations, parties and counsel often will behave poorly and engage in conduct destructive to the negotiation process. Threats to walk away, assertions of lack of authority, nonnegotiable demands, and intimidation are just a few examples of the tactics or tricks that can derail direct negotiations between parties. In our experience, the mere presence of a mediator usually alters such behavior. In a mediation, parties and counsel are usually on good behavior as they want to convince the mediator that their conduct giving rise to the dispute was not responsible for it. They also want to convince the mediator that their approaches to the negotiations are both fair and reasonable. In any event, the mediator is in a far better position than the parties to develop approaches and strategies that minimize the significance of such tactics.

5.2.11 Poor Negotiating Skills, including Failing to Understand the "Other Side"

Well over 90 percent of all cases in litigation are resolved prior to trial. While most litigators are well trained in advocacy and trial skills, they approach negotiations on a somewhat intuitive basis. It is not at all surprising, therefore, that many lawyers find it difficult to resolve a case until the ultimate imperative arrives—the looming trial date.

Parties and counsel often approach settlement negotiations with a firm view of what they want or need but without any consideration of what they might have to accept—their bottom line. One of the most important and effective negotiation tools is first striving to understand what the other party needs and trying to meet needs that are consistent with one's own. Parties and counsel commonly make a thorough analysis of their own rights and interests but often fail to make a significant analysis of the other side's perspectives and interests. In most negotiations, advocates are far too focused on trying to convince the other side of the strength of their positions and insufficiently attentive to what the other side is saying. Many parties are unwilling to make a significant move in a negotiation because they subscribe to the conventional wisdom that "a party should not bid against itself."

Most highly skilled mediators are well versed in the art and science of negotiations. Training and experience permit a skilled mediator to assist parties with their negotiating strategies and decisions. For example, a skilled mediator will explain that appreciating what the other side wants is an important first step in finding common ground. In addition, notwithstanding the conventional wisdom that parties should not bid against themselves, a skilled mediator can show parties how they can anchor a negotiation in *their* zone by making what is considered the first credible offer. Mediators can also set a stage for parties to listen to each other carefully and respectfully. As suggested earlier, mediators can urge parties to make more objective evaluations and to compare proposals not to abstract wish lists but to the consequences should settlement negotiations fail.

5.2.12 Inappropriate Reliance on Experts

In many disputes, parties develop hardline positions in negotiations due to a heavy reliance on their own experts. This can happen at two different stages.

First, business disputes, especially in highly complex and technical industries, often can involve differences of opinion about technical issues. Think of an argument over whether or not one party met the manufacturing specifications of a supply agreement, or whether or not a vaccine will be approved by a governmental authority. In such cases, a party's internal experts will have taken a position that they believe in and/or is difficult for them to relinquish without losing face within the company as critical decisions—to terminate a contract, for example—will have been taken based upon their views. Hiring a joint external expert may be suggested by the mediator to help address such disputes and achieve some degree of objectivity.

In later stages, if a case has progressed to litigation or arbitration, given the late stage in the litigation process at which expert reports are exchanged, parties can be unaware for years of the positions of their adversary's experts. A skilled mediator can provide for an early, informal exchange of opinions by these outside experts. These exchanges can occur even before experts have formed their final opinions or offered their written reports. In several cases, Ben has conducted what can be characterized as a "minitrial within a mediation." These mediations featured an informal, mediator-moderated exchange of experts' opinions, where the experts have had a limited opportunity to state their conclusions and to pose questions to each other. In these minitrials, attorneys and clients attending the mediation have merely observed this controlled exchange. A mediator with technical expertise can use her background to probe parties on technical issues. In each case, the opportunity to observe an exchange of the views of experts or hear from an industry expert has resulted in a softening of hardline settlement positions and served as a predicate to resolution.

5.2.13 Preoccupation With Winning and the Litigator Mindset

Success in a business mediation requires a willingness to compromise, look forward, and avoid focusing on accountability or righting a wrong. It also requires a willingness to share information voluntarily to fill information gaps. Although persuading the other side that there is risk for them and preparing your arguments is important, focusing on "winning" the mediation by vanquishing the other side or viewing the goal of the exercise as to persuade the mediator of the truth of one's views will quickly backfire.

Many companies commence litigation based upon a belief that they have been wronged in a commercial transaction. Upon being served with a complaint, many companies perceive that they have been wrongfully attacked and may be tempted, at least initially, to adopt a win-at-any-cost approach. Business people directly involved in the transaction at the core of the litigation often urge their key executives to seek a declaration of rights in order to be vindicated. This attitude often poisons mediations. While many larger companies have institutionalized pre-litigation dispute resolution techniques, the support from within may not be very broad nor very deep. Moreover, smaller and more entrepreneurial companies that rarely are involved in litigation are even less inclined to compromise (at least initially) and often view the need to prosecute or defend a suit to be a matter of principle.

Counsel hired to represent clients in businesses litigations may not initially focus on the probability of a negotiated settlement and gear up for battle—bringing to the table a litigator's mindset—thereby exacerbating a client's tendencies.

As previously noted, these types of reactions of companies and their counsel are strong arguments to mediate before a litigation or arbitration is filed.

In mediation, a skilled mediator can get the parties to recognize that not every case should be interpreted as a matter of principle. As one legal analyst stated: "Every case is a matter of 'principle' until the client receives the third and fourth bill from outside counsel at which time, they will begin to spell the word differently ('principal')."

In addition, a skilled mediator often will be successful in convincing parties that they need to focus not on what happened, but on the evidence a court will hear. While parties often want to litigate to establish the truth, a skilled mediator can suggest why they can hope only for "court truth" as distinct from "absolute truth." Ultimately, the mediator's challenge is to urge the parties to take a more bottom-line approach in pursuit of their claims and defenses. By examining all the relevant considerations and viewing the dispute as a problem to be solved, most parties—and their counsel—will realize that their most responsible decision will be one that involves some compromise.

5.2.14 Inability to Break Impasse

Parties who elect to engage in the process of direct and unassisted negotiations often find it difficult to overcome an impasse on their own. Skilled mediators recognize the first signals of approaching impasse when they hear statements such as "This is my bottom line," "I knew this would be a waste of time," or "We are leaving." A skilled mediator can also detect early signs of possible impasse from the nonverbal conduct of the parties. Skilled mediators are particularly adept at determining whether the impasse is a matter of posturing or whether it is real. If the perceived impasse occurs as a consequence of posturing between the parties or by a party with the mediator, mediators use a number of techniques to generate movement and overcome the problem. Even when a real and ultimate impasse occurs, skilled mediators are well versed in a number of impasse-breaking techniques, for example, adjournment, requesting a "last best" offer proposal, or using a double-blind, "mediator's" proposal. In such an instance, the proposal is made to each side confidentially for their acceptance or rejection. Unless both accept, a party will not know whether the other side has accepted the proposal.

5.2.15 Process Barriers

Each of the above paragraphs illuminates the barriers to resolution in party-to-party negotiations and the ways in which a mediator can overcome them. In addition to the techniques, skills, and strategies that a mediator brings to the process, the simple fact that there is an event, or as we like to refer to it, a process—the mediation itself—enhances the potential for resolution.

In many cases, parties are simply not ready to resolve a dispute in direct negotiations because of their need for a day in court. Mediation can provide the needed day in court by giving the parties an opportunity to tell their story and get feedback from a neutral. This does not have to happen in an opening session; it can happen in written submissions or at any point during live mediation sessions. Moreover, in mediation, parties are better prepared for negotiations and are required to make decisions within a defined time frame. Further, in direct negotiations, parties often need approval to settle at levels beyond their authorization or are concerned about the need for cover in order that their settlement decisions not be criticized at higher levels within the organization. Recommendations or feedback from a mediator often can satisfy these needs and concerns. Finally, in direct negotiations, it is easy to blame the other side for any failure to achieve resolution. In contrast, parties in mediation are likely to become invested in the process and work harder to achieve a resolution; achieving resolution becomes a part of the definition of success.

5.3 Conclusion

Whatever the barriers to resolution, good mediators bring to the table an understanding of the social psychology of negotiations and an appreciation for how parties perceive and deal with the issue of risk. Highly skilled mediators are well versed in mediation techniques like paraphrasing, framing, and the use of mediator transparency. They also know how to manage the process when a party is not acting in good faith or where there is an imbalance of power. The best mediators apply leadership and problem-solving skills and earn the trust of the parties.

Mediators with significant transactional experience and industry expertise can use these additional tools and credibility with the business to help the parties think about how they got into their dispute and how to solve it, modifying their perception of perceived facts based upon their own experience with similar transactions.

Ultimately, all good mediators will involve the parties directly in the search for solutions. While direct and unassisted negotiation should remain the initial path to dispute resolution, where some of the above barriers appear to be an impediment, parties should recognize the benefits of a facilitated negotiation and a possible evaluation with the help of a skilled and experienced mediator.

Chapter 6
Preparation

6.1 Introduction

In order to take full advantage of the opportunities presented by mediation, the mediation advocate and participating business representatives need to understand the mediation process and be completely prepared. Indeed, over the years we have come to believe that in significant business disputes, the work that parties do internally and with each other before getting together, guided by the suggestions of the mediator, is just as or even more important than the live joint sessions typically thought of as the mediation. The mediation, in other words, involves all of the steps taken to get to an amicable resolution, including preparation itself.

In the past, since mediation is non-binding, many attorneys erroneously assumed that there is no downside and that the preparation needed for a mediation was minimal. In fact, significant information exchange and process design by the parties and their counsel is critical to the success of the process overall, no matter when mediation is contemplated. Good preparation is as much a key to success in mediation as it is in litigation.

The implications of this for business clients, particularly inside counsel, cannot be overstated. Heading into a mediation, they should work to ensure that the business takes the process seriously and is prepared to make an upfront investment to resolve the matter. Mediation counsel should be prepared to explain the benefits of this investment and put aside strategic concerns about strategically withholding information that will come out in a litigation or arbitration eventually anyway.

This need to focus on upfront investment becomes even more acute at a point where mediation can, with the right preparation, be the most effective—before a litigation or arbitration is filed. At this point, a more business-focused approach may be easier because the litigation/arbitration apparatus, which generally exacerbates conflict, has not been engaged.

This chapter suggests strategies that will enable mediation counsel and business representatives to maximize the opportunities offered by mediation. Throughout, counsel and their clients should view the likely conversation with the other side and the mediator as occurring on two distinct tracks: first, an assessment of the likelihood of success in a litigation or arbitration, and second, a preferred business solution even assuming, for the sake of argument, that an adjudication outcome is more likely than not to be successful for the business. A compromise business solution may well be in a client's interest given the protracted cost and distraction of achieving what might in the end feel like a Pyrrhic victory.

6.2 Step-by-Step Mediation Analysis

The chart on the following page provides an overview of the mediation process. From the outset of a dispute, counsel should take a view of the big picture—the entire mediation process—in order to take full advantage of the process.

6.3 Make an Objective Litigation/Arbitration Risk Analysis

To determine the business negotiating strategy in mediation and establish benchmarks for settlement, counsel and business representatives should assess the likely outcomes and probable costs of a dispute in litigation (or arbitration). Any such risk analysis should include the following assessments:

- Evaluate the reasons that the dispute arose—are external factors such as a break in a third-party supply chain the problem? Were the objectives in a collaboration insufficiently defined? Was one party technically incapable of fulfilling its contractual obligations? Objective assessments of why the dispute arose in the first place are critical to assessing the case and to the assessment of interests outlined in the next section. It is important to include in this assessment reasonably objective business executives who are not "on the line" in connection with what is now a "problem."
- If in a pre-litigation situation, are there other related claims or legal problems that may surface in connection with the dispute on the table?
- Strengths and weaknesses of a client's case, including assessment of legal arguments and the credibility of witnesses and evidence.
- Evaluate the strengths and weaknesses of opponent's case.

- Determine the best and worst possible outcomes of a litigated or arbitrated resolution (consider a decision tree approach to this analysis, which emphasizes an assessment of the cumulative risk of winning or losing as discussed in the last chapter).

identify problem and nature of dispute

⇩

assess facts, claims, defenses, damages

⇩

evaluate business goals, objectives, interests and needs

⇩

evaluate other party's goals, objectives, interests and needs

⇩

perform arbitration or litigation risk and cost analysis

⇩

consider all dispute resolution alternatives:
negotiation? litigation? mediation? other options?

⇩

determine suitability for mediation

⇩

propose mediation to adverse party

⇩

design mediation process

⇩

select mediator

⇩

complete design of mediation process

⇩

ensure buy-in from internal stakeholders on settlement options

⇩

implement preparation steps with other parties and mediator

⇩

attend live mediation sessions

⇩	⇩
resolution	dispute continues
⇩	⇩
⇩	⇩
prepare written settlement agreement if parties resolve dispute	consider alternatives if mediation does not resolve dispute

Figure 6.1 Overview of the Mediation Process

- Transparent and realistic estimate client costs of litigation, including discovery, motions, witness preparation, expert fees, and trial costs, as well as the cost of appeals of an adverse result.
- Consider the transactional costs to client, including time away from the conduct of normal business, impact on morale, and loss of productivity.
- Assess the probable timelines in litigation, including any appeals and the willingness of the client's leadership (at a variety of levels, particularly in a large corporation) to support a lengthy process.
- Assess the financial condition of the adverse party and determine whether there are any collectability problems.

6.4 Analyze the Interests of All Parties

The underlying interests often are as compelling as—and sometimes more compelling than—the rights and obligations of the parties when making a settlement analysis and developing a negotiating strategy for mediation. We noted above the need for a clearheaded, objective assessment of why the dispute arose, and this should constitute the basis for an assessment of interests, as well. Following on from this, any analysis of the underlying interests should also include the following assessments:

- What are the goals and objectives of the client? What does the client really need?
- What are the goals and objectives of all other parties? What do they really need?
- Do the underlying interests present any specific reason why mediation (or early resolution) may be particularly attractive?
- Is there any need or potential to preserve a relationship or take into account the possibility of a future relationship given the industry?
- Does any party have a particular need for confidentiality?
- Does the existence of the dispute create a morale problem for any party?
- Does the pending dispute create an impediment to a party's strategic plans over the next two to three years?
- What impact will a settlement have on a company's bottom line? On its reported earnings? On a division's budget?
- What issues are most important to each party? Least important?

6.5 Discuss the Decision to Mediate

In evaluating whether a dispute should be mediated (see section 2.2), counsel and business representatives should explore the following questions with the client:

- Is a settlement possible?
- What are the likely barriers to a settlement?
- Is it too soon for settlement to occur? What is the basis for this belief, and can these concerns be addressed in the mediation process?
- Is more information required before a settlement decision can be made and, if so, can the parties agree to exchange this information as part of a mediation agreement?
- Are there other claims or potential disputes not yet involved in the case or controversy that can also be resolved in a mediation?
- Are emotions or hostilities likely to bar the kind of communication necessary to settle a dispute? If so, is it possible that the mediation will provide an appropriate forum for better communication?
- Are there additional stakeholders in the dispute that may be willing to participate in settlement discussions?
- Are all parties to the dispute willing to engage in a good-faith effort to resolve the dispute?

Once the answers to these questions have been reviewed, the client can review the factors outlined in 2.2 and make an informed decision about whether mediation will best serve its interests.

6.6 Select the Mediator

6.6.1 General Considerations

After making the decision to mediate, counsel should determine what type of mediator is best suited for the client and the particular dispute. Counsel should then find the candidate with the appropriate expertise, style, and other desired qualities. Each party may submit a list of candidates for the opponent's review, or the parties may retain a neutral dispute resolution service to recommend a mediator for their consideration. Among the organizations prepared to recommend mediator candidates in business disputes are the CPR Institute, the AAA, and JAMS. Organizations such as the American College of Civil Trial Mediators and the International Academy of Mediators also offer, on their websites, the credentials of mediators highly skilled and experienced in mediating commercial disputes. When turning to an organization to administer the selection process, parties should inform the organization of any preferences in mediation style, experience, expertise, or location of candidates.

Counsel should take the selection process seriously and take the time to engage in due diligence. A competent advocate should learn as much as possible about mediator candidates by obtaining their credentials and references, researching community reputation, and speaking to the candidates directly. It is entirely appropriate to ask candidates specific questions about their experience, style, and expertise (see section 4.2).

Selection should be directly tied to the outcome the business client wants or thinks is possible. If the renegotiation of a business arrangement is contemplated or if an evaluation of "commercially reasonable efforts" or compliance with regulatory requirements tied to a warranty may be desirable, a mediator with transactional, industry, and/or technical expertise may be required. A mediator who does not have substantial direct contract negotiation experience may not have as many tools to help the parties as a former litigator. The ability to speak the language of business and quickly grasp the industry context may also be critical to the success of the mediation.

Since initial private conversations with a mediator candidate may create the appearance of bias, especially if there are lengthy conversations of substance, it may be advisable to schedule an initial joint conference with a mediator candidate and opposing counsel for the purpose of interviewing a particular candidate.

The following factors should be considered in the selection process:

- Personal qualities of an effective mediator (see section 4.2)
- Mediation style and approach
  - Facilitative or evaluative
  - Broad or narrow
  - Passive or active
  - Combined
- Expertise/previous roles—what type and why in relationship to the desired outcome?
  - Subject matter
  - Specific industry
  - Inside counsel roles
  - Transactional (as opposed to only former litigator)

  - Business experience
  - Technical experience (e.g., engineering, biology/chemistry)
  - Legal experience
- Mediation experience
- Availability of mediator
- The mediator's professional fees and administrative charges
- How and when the mediator uses caucus sessions
- Whether the mediator encourages lawyer participation
- Whether the mediator will involve the parties directly
- Whether the mediator can credibly discuss industry practices, regulations, and laws based upon direct experience
- How the mediator uses reality-testing techniques
- The circumstances in which the mediator will offer an evaluative opinion
- Whether the mediator requires pre-mediation documentation and submissions
- Any conflict of interest or reason the mediator may not be absolutely impartial
- Restrictions on future representations if mediator is a practicing lawyer
- References from lawyers and parties in similar disputes

Once the mediator is selected, the parties should enter into a written agreement with the mediator covering issues such as the mediation process, confidentiality, conflicts of interest, and pricing. The topic of confidentiality is particularly important as laws vary from state to state and in federal courts as to whether or not the entire mediation process, from intake through settlement, is confidential. It is a best practice to establish contractual obligations of strict confidentiality among all participants, including the mediator.

6.6.2 Increasing Diversity in the Mediation Profession

This section would not be complete if we did not urge those choosing mediators to recognize that there are numerous highly qualified, diverse mediators practicing today, as well as the resulting benefits to participants arising from the selection of diverse neutrals. This is particularly important given that in recent years, mediators (and arbitrators) serve a role that often is a substitute for judicial process.

In 2018, at the initiative of its Women in Dispute Resolution Committee, but with the help of many others in connection with research, report drafting, and implementation, the American Bar Association (ABA) Dispute Resolution Section proposed, and the ABA passed, Resolution 105:

> RESOLVED, That the American Bar Association urges providers of domestic and international dispute resolution to expand their rosters with minorities, women, persons with disabilities, and persons of differing sexual orientations and gender identities ("diverse neutrals") and to encourage the selection of diverse neutrals; and
>
> FURTHER RESOLVED, That the American Bar Association urges all users of domestic and international legal and neutral services to select and use diverse neutrals.[14]

As summarized in the accompanying report supporting the resolution (footnote omitted):

> This Resolution addresses elimination of bias and enhancing diversity in Dispute Resolution—a segment of "legal" services that has been described as "arguably the least diverse corner of the profession . . ." [T]he available data show that diversity within Dispute Resolution significantly lags the legal profession as a whole. Despite significant efforts on the part of institutional providers of dispute resolution services to increase the diversity of their rosters, diverse neutrals remain underrepresented (the "roster issue"). The roster issue is compounded by the fact that qualified diverse neutrals are less likely to be selected due to the network-based and confidential nature of the profession, which in combination, results in selection of neutrals taking place in relative obscurity, enabling implicit bias to play a greater role in selection (the "selection problem"). This lack of transparency also undermines potential efforts to address the selection problem. By leaving recommendations and referrals largely in the hands of outside counsel and established neutrals, it reduces the role that clients can play in addressing the problem by including Dispute Resolution in their larger efforts to improve diversity in the legal profession. In addition, the lack of transparency reduces public awareness of lack of diversity in Dispute Resolution, and thus also reduces the incentive of stakeholders such as outside counsel, institutional service providers and

14. See https://www.americanbar.org/groups/dispute_resolution/resources/aba-resolution-105/.

established neutrals to take proactive steps without client pressure. By raising awareness of the lack of diversity in Dispute Resolution, the proposed resolution will encourage all stakeholders to take action.[15]

What specific action steps can be taken by those who recognize the important values and benefits of diversity? Those selecting mediators should have greater top of the mind awareness when selecting a mediator to overcome the forces of inertia and implicit bias. We have found that many individuals who fully support diversity initiatives in other areas have not necessarily considered the problems that exist in the mediation and arbitration field. Advocates selecting neutrals should not simply rely upon the patters of yesteryear and send an email to colleagues that invariably begins, "Can anyone recommend a mediator . . . ?" The replies will reflect the past and not the present. And again, there is a deep and talented pool of diverse neutrals available for selection today. The business clients in commercial disputes, often General Counsel or company executives, can demand of their outside law firms—through the selection of diverse neutrals—and track compliance in the same way that they make demands and track compliance, more generally, of the law firms representing them.

Resources relating to ABA Resolution 105, including the list of action steps prepared by the ABA Dispute Resolution Section in connection with Resolution 105, are available in our bibliography. The major arbitration and mediation institutions, including the CPR Institute, the AAA, JAMS, and international organizations such as the International Chamber of Commerce (ICC) are all quite focused on this topic and can assist with diverse neutral selection.

Only when women, persons of color, and other diverse mediators are selected on a regular basis will the participants served in mediations be enriched by the experiences, perspectives, and wisdom that will result from their selection.

6.7 Participate With Mediator in Designing the Process

The mediator, especially in more substantial or complex disputes, can and should assist counsel in preparing for a successful process. For example, the mediator can help determine what type of negotiating approach will be most effective, whether to have experts attend the mediation sessions, or

15. See https://www.americanbar.org/groups/dispute_resolution/resources/aba-resolution-105/.

whether visual aids might be helpful. While *ex parte* contacts are entirely appropriate, it is important that they be disclosed in a general way and balanced overall in order that the mediator be perceived by the parties as absolutely impartial.

The availability of secure and flexible virtual mediation modalities has expanded the list of considerations in designing the overall process (see section 3.3).

These are the important procedural issues to discuss with the mediator:

- Dates and times (with attention to time zone differences)
- Will the live sessions proceed virtually, in-person, or in some combination of the two, and if virtual, will more time be needed to accommodate "Zoom fatigue" and more breaks from screen time (possibly split over two days)
- Location and available facilities for in-person sessions; technical aspects and protocols for virtual sessions
- Anticipated length of process
- Exchange of key documents with the mediator and between the parties to serve as common reference points and other information on facts, claims, and defenses (contracts, amendments, emails, expert analysis, previous direct negotiating correspondence, insurance policies, etc.); particularly important for pre-litigation mediations, but always helpful
- Necessary participants, and whether those individuals are available for in-person sessions versus only virtual sessions
- Written submissions—exchanges between the parties (especially important for pre-litigation or arbitration), as well as confidential submissions to the mediator only
- Ex parte calls with the mediator prior to live sessions to discuss information and written submissions
- Practice sessions for virtual mediations or those participating virtually
- Oral presentations during live sessions
- Administrative and professional fees
- Confidentiality

In planning for the mediation sessions, the participants should set aside sufficient time. We have found that parties routinely underestimate the amount of time to invest in a robust—and successful—mediation process. "We only want one day," is a common refrain. It is not uncommon in the mediation of a dispute involving substantial dollars or interests, however, for the initial process to take a significant number of hours of preparation and two days or longer for live sessions and for follow-up sessions as necessary. This is particularly true in cases in which a litigation has not been filed. In complex commercial cases, mediators commonly will ask the participants to set aside two or more consecutive days for the initial live sessions and to be prepared to stay into the evenings, if necessary. Virtual sessions may need to take place over more time to avoid the effects of Zoom fatigue and to address time zone differences.

6.8 Preparation

6.8.1 Importance of Preparation, including Information Exchange

Preparation is essential for an effective mediation process. Lawyers and parties often participate in a mediation without a full understanding of the dispute or the process. With good preparation, parties and their counsel can significantly enhance the likelihood of a positive outcome. Going even further, we believe that the concept of "the mediation" as a whole should not emphasize merely the in-person or live virtual joint sessions but rather focus just as much on the various phases of a mediation process that consist of preparation steps, including exchanges of information between the parties, leading up to one or more in-person or joint virtual sessions, and any necessary follow-up. Simply put, the mediation starts with the first planning call and continues through all of the phases until the parties decide that further contact in a mediation process is not fruitful or should continue only in parallel with other processes.

6.8.2 Comparison of Preparation for Mediation with Preparation for Litigation

Preparation for a mediation is different from preparing for a deposition or a trial. The following important differences should be considered when preparing for a mediation:

- *Role of the client.* Unlike litigation or arbitration, in a business mediation, the client is directly involved and plays a pivotal role. The client, therefore, should also be central in the preparation stage. The client needs to be prepared for its role as a presenter of information, a negotiator, and a decision maker. Particularly in a business dispute, the more the process can feel like a normal business negotiation rather than a litigation battle, the more likely the mediation is to be a success. Ideally, the participants involved should to some extent mirror the participants in a negotiated deal. Consider having inside counsel, transactional lawyers, and non-legal business representatives lead the way, with outside counsel litigators in the background.

- *Appropriate outside counsel representative.* While it would be inappropriate to send an outside counsel, corporate department, deal lawyer to defend a deposition, it may make infinite sense to have such an attorney function as co-lead or lead client representative in the mediation process. This will depend on the potential settlement options. If a nonmonetary arrangement may be on the table, transactional lawyers have more experience with the rhythm of business negotiations and with drafting business arrangements than litigators do. Litigators should always be involved to some extent, however, as what might be acceptable as a compromise is always to some extent related to legal risk.
- *Legal and business "discovery."* If information is necessary to evaluate the merits of the case or reasonable settlement options, counsel should determine how such information should be obtained and whether formal discovery is really necessary. The mediator—especially in a pre-litigation mediation, but increasingly always—will urge the parties to voluntarily exchange information that is important for each side to assess its legal and business position. For example, defendants often are unprepared to resolve claims in mediation without having received damage information. The business ability of a party to meet contractual obligations in the future, even if there have been problems in the past, constituting grounds for breach or possible termination, may also be important data points for any business solution. The mediator's assistance should be enlisted in the event an agreement on voluntary exchange cannot be obtained. We note that this process should be tailored to the amount in dispute and emphasize getting enough information to make an intelligent decision about how to proceed.
- *Mediation position paper exchanges.* Written exchanges between the parties and the mediator give each side the ability to explain their latest thinking about the merits and possible settlement options in their own words and avoid the need for a potentially inflammatory opening statement during live sessions. It also makes the live sessions more efficient by ameliorating the need for the mediator to first explain the

other sides' position and only then move on to reality testing and helping the parties negotiate a solution. These types of exchanges are especially important in a pre-litigation mediation session given the lack of a complaint/demand and answer/response but are usually helpful to some reasonable extent for any mediation, regardless of the procedural posture of the case. They should be drafted in a matter-of-fact, professional way to avoid needlessly antagonizing the recipient.

Confidential submissions to the mediator afford an opportunity to convince the mediator of the correctness of a client's position or the reasonableness of a particular settlement option using information they would not like to share with the other side at the outset. These submissions also afford an opportunity to address the client's underlying interests and objectives. They also should be drafted with care and professionalism.

- *Rules of evidence*. Rules of evidence do not apply in mediation. There is no formal direct or cross-examination of witnesses. A mediator may, however, request that a party explain his or her statements and perspectives or react to what an opponent has asserted. Witness interviews and preparation, therefore, are as important in mediation as they are in litigation. And if the next step after an unsuccessful mediation is a court proceeding, whether or not a particular piece of evidence is admissible under the applicable rules may be an important part of the assessment of legal risk. This should be directly addressed with the mediator.
- *Formal, live mediation sessions*. In preparing legal arguments or settlement proposals to be presented at the mediation session or sessions, counsel should recognize that the process affords an opportunity to make presentations to representatives of the parties as well as to the mediator. This approach is different from litigation, in which statements are addressed to a judge or jury.
- *Negotiations*. Mediation, as a negotiating process, is perforce a much less adversarial and more cooperative process than litigation. While arguments should be presented persuasively, counsel and the business representatives should avoid the use of emotionally charged language and should acknowledge the other parties' concerns, where appropriate. At times, the atmosphere of a mediation is not unlike an oral argument in court and, at times, not unlike the negotiation of a business deal. As we have stressed, emphasizing the latter can be important to a

successful resolution, and openly acknowledging which track is being discussed—litigation/arbitration risk versus a business solution—can be helpful in avoiding unproductive hostility.

6.8.3 Identify the Client Representatives Who Should Participate

To maximize the opportunities presented by mediation, it is important to identify the client representatives who will take ownership of the dispute. While the participation of individuals with knowledge of facts giving rise to a controversy may or may not advance the client's interests, it is more important to encourage the participation of a decision maker with full authority to make resolution decisions, including the impact any such decision may have on a division's budget or the company's reported earnings. Counsel should make every effort to identify and encourage the appropriate client representatives to participate in mediation in order to have the best opportunity to recognize potential solutions and to ensure that any settlement decision is made with full appreciation of the risks and likely outcomes in litigation. The availability of virtual participation is helpful, but if the main session is in-person, the decision makers should be present.

If there is any chance that the mediated settlement will involve the negotiation of terms other than money, it is highly recommended that transactional representatives for the client—such as corporate transactional counsel and business development—are present or available for the sessions. Similarly, the outside law firm may want to tap its corporate department for participation in the mediation.

6.8.4 Client Representatives Ensure Internal Stakeholder Engagement

In larger corporations, it may not be possible or necessary to secure the direct participation in live sessions of all the stakeholders who will need to sign off on a settlement, particularly if the resolution will involve business terms in addition to or other than pure dollars. If this is the case, throughout the preparation process, it is critical that the participating client representatives are working with others in their company to make sure that all of the functions that will need to have input—finance, manufacturing, marketing, etc.—are aligned on the negotiating plan. Securing such participation in the mediated outcome can be one of the key roles played by participating inside counsel, for example.

6.8.5 Consider Alternatives to a Negotiated Agreement (BATNA and WATNA)

Before beginning formal negotiations, counsel should help the client explore alternatives should negotiations fail—the BATNA and WATNA, the "best" and "worst" alternatives to a negotiated agreement. These concepts have been around since the 1980s, and in our view, they have absolutely withstood the test of time. Parties return to them again and again for guidance in thinking about their most informed negotiated decision.[16] By examining various alternatives, the business representatives and counsel can jointly determine whether or not any settlement being offered in mediation is in the client's best interests. A viable, well-developed alternative to a negotiated settlement gives the client the power to negotiate from a position of strength. Counsel should specifically assist the client in determining its BATNA. Any offer that is better than a party's BATNA should be accepted.

Assessing whether the opposing party has a strong or weak BATNA also helps in understanding its position and negotiating strengths. The more the advocate knows about his or her opponent's alternatives, the better prepared he or she is to negotiate a successful resolution.

Counsel should also assist the client in developing its WATNA. Defining the WATNA protects the client from accepting an inadequate settlement offer. Used in conjunction with the BATNA, it is another tool for recognizing when to accept or reject a settlement offer. Having worked out the BATNA and WATNA prior to negotiations, the advocate will have more control throughout the mediation process. At the same time, however, parties should be open to the possibility that their BATNA and WATNA can change as a result of what they learn in the mediation process.

6.8.6 Prepare Arguments Supporting Legal Positions and Settlement Proposals—Track 1

Counsel should prepare arguments supporting the merits of claims and defenses in the same manner as when preparing for trial, even in a prelitigation or arbitration mediation. This analysis is by nature a retrospective look at the past. Counsel should be able to demonstrate to the mediator and opposing parties the strengths of the client's case and weaknesses of the opponent's case. Counsel should also prepare in advance any reason

16. *See* ROGER FISHER AND WILLIAM URY, GETTING TO YES: NEGOTIATING AGREEMENT WITHOUT GIVING IN (1981).

why the other side should be willing to move to a "reasonable" settlement proposal. Here, the advocate's goal is to persuade the other side to consider his or her client's proposal. Accordingly, counsel should recognize and be prepared to advance reasons why the other side's interests are being served by a specific settlement proposal.

6.8.7 Explore Creative Business Solutions—Track 2

To remain open to creative solutions, the mediation advocate and her client should look at the case from the holistic business perspective of all parties. This is the second track of any robust business mediation—the possibility of a business solution that resolves a dispute early, even assuming hypothetically that a client's litigation/legal case is strong. Here, the focus is on the future. Together with the client, counsel should determine the interests, objectives, concerns, and needs of each party. Brainstorming with the client will enhance the possibility of recognizing possible creative solutions that work for all parties to the dispute and help everyone get back to the business of business and away from the business of litigation.

6.8.8 Prepare for Client's Direct Involvement

Since clients often become directly involved in the mediation process, they must be fully prepared for this role. Counsel should meet with the representatives of the client to discuss the mediation process, the client's involvement, and issues such as format, procedure, demeanor, and dress. Any virtual mediation will require more upfront preparation with the client as discussed earlier in this book, and rehearsal sessions to ensure that the client is comfortable with the setting, to discuss how breakout rooms work, and to confirm that their internet connection, lighting, and sound are optimal. In short, the representative of the client should know what to expect so that the client is at ease and well prepared for his or her role as a presenter of information and a negotiator.

6.8.9 Decide Who Should Take the Lead in Sessions

Counsel and the client representative should determine together who should take the lead role during the mediation sessions—the advocate (and whether that lead advocate should be a litigator, transactional representative, or inside counsel) or the client representative. To make this determination, counsel should consider the client representative's sophistication, ability to articulate goals, knowledge of the subject matter, ability for constructive expression, and the advisability of the client's active participation. If the client representative is a persuasive and effective communicator, the client has an advantage that should be used in the mediation. It is also important to recognize that the client's participation gives the adverse party a preview of how well the client representative will perform as a witness in court. In general, the more a client participates, the more satisfied the client will be with the process and the outcome, and the more the entire process will feel like a business negotiation rather than a litigation process.

6.8.10 Explore Potential for Collaborative Negotiations

Whether negotiating directly with an adversary or in a mediation setting, movement often depends on the willingness of the parties to cooperate. For example, counsel should consider what information needs to be exchanged to evaluate reasonable settlement options. Counsel may then agree voluntarily to exchange such information. Working with the opposing party in a cooperative manner demonstrates the advocate's and the client's good-faith commitment to the process of a negotiated resolution.

Though the mediation advocate should be committed to a good-faith effort to resolve the dispute, he or she nevertheless must represent the client energetically and persuasively. The advocate should argue convincingly on behalf of the client and be cautious of compromising too much too soon. However, in mediation, the lawyer must balance zealous advocacy with good negotiating techniques. Counsel should understand the interests and goals of his or her client and the opposing party. Counsel also should avoid emotional language in an effort to minimize antagonism and to create a path for settlement.

6.8.11 Develop a Negotiating Plan

Whether the parties are engaged in a pure dollars dispute or one that involves the potential for a business solution, counsel and the client should prepare a negotiating plan in advance of the mediation sessions based upon the hopefully robust preparation encouraged by the mediator. All too often, parties lose significant advantages in mediation as the result of having planned only initial offers and demands and tentative final positions.

Many mediations begin with the parties taking extreme positions, often representing the last offers and demands in settlement negotiations proceeding the mediation. Initially, parties often find themselves at an impasse as the result of their unwillingness to bid against themselves. In these circumstances, counsel should consider the advantages of making the first credible move. Even a small move, if credible, may enable the mediator to meet with the other side and gain significant concessions (see section 7.4.5).

In recognition of the fact that counsel and the client will be engaged in a kind of negotiation with the mediator as well as with adverse parties, counsel should plan the extent of voluntary candor they will use with the mediator. The degree of voluntary candor may depend on a number of factors, including whether the mediator is more facilitative or evaluative; whether the communication involves legal arguments, underlying business interests, or settlement positions; and whether the mediation is in its early or late stages. In the final analysis, this judgment call is likely to depend on the level of comfort with the mediator and be made in the fluid environment of the mediation sessions.

In developing a negotiating plan, counsel should consider the following:

- Litigation risk and cost–benefit analysis
- Client's interests, goals, and objectives
- Both sides' BATNA and WATNA
- The other side's business operations and corporate culture
- Possible creative paths toward settlement
- Possible collaborative negotiating strategies
- Client's opening position
- Advantage of first credible move
- Offers contingent upon movement by the other side
- Possible counteroffers and responses
- Rationale to support negotiating positions
- Preparation of chart for tracking offers and counteroffers during negotiations
- Suggestions for mediator in event of impasse
- Plan for negotiating with mediator

While a specific negotiating plan is essential, counsel and the client should recognize the need for flexibility in the mediation sessions and should be prepared to reevaluate the plan in light of new information received and the mediator's suggestions.

6.8.12 Avoid Irrational Attachment to Positions

When preparing for mediation, most parties establish benchmarks for settlement in advance of the process. In disputes primarily about money, after assessing the likely risks and costs of litigation, as well as the possibility that value may be contributed through business solutions other than cash, most parties identify settlement ranges, and many establish "bottom lines." Invariably, these assessments are influenced by irrational attachments to positions, sometimes referred to as cognitive illusions, which produce errors in judgment that impact settlement decisions. Parties and counsel, therefore, when establishing benchmarks for settlement, should make every effort to determine whether any of the following cognitive illusions (or biases) have affected their evaluations or decisions about settlement:

- *Risk/loss aversion.* Studies on negotiation have established that parties make different decisions about risk depending on whether they categorize (or frame) the risk as a gain or a loss. Usually from the reference point of the status quo, most parties are risk-averse when protecting settlements regarded as gains and are risk-seeking when making decisions involving results regarded as losses. For example, most plaintiffs would prefer receiving $100,000 (a gain) to a 50 percent chance of a verdict of $200,000. On the other hand, most defendants would prefer a 50 percent chance of a verdict of $200,000 to a payment (or a loss) of $100,000. And, as we have discussed, another way to explain this aversion is to note that anyone, regardless of what side of the *v.* they are on, finds the experience of perceived loss very painful. As mediated settlements require each side to give up their assessment of what they think is the right result and move their sunk litigation costs, they almost create serious feelings of loss for both sides.[17]
- *Advocacy, confirmation, and assimilation bias; cognitive dissonance.* Most parties and counsel have difficulty overcoming self-serving judgments about the likelihood of success on the merits in litigation (or arbitration). The bias results from selective perception and assimilation bias (the tendency of many people to see or hear only information that favors their own position) and the fact that most parties identify the strengths of their case but pay insufficient attention to or discredit possible weaknesses. In one study on advocacy bias, given the same set of facts and an instruction to make an objective evaluation of a case in order to provide the client with a benchmark to assist in making settlement decisions, participating "plaintiffs" found in favor of plaintiffs and

17. See Mediating Legal Disputes, Chapter 6.

for substantially higher amounts than did participating "defendants." Overall, cognitive dissonance plays a role as well.

- *Certainty bias.* Studies on negotiations have established that most people overestimate their degree of certainty when answering questions or making assessments about probable outcomes in litigation. As a group, lawyers are particularly likely to overestimate their degree of certainty. This bias should be examined when making settlement recommendations and decisions, particularly when predicting the likely result at trial on a percentage basis. Given the uncertainty in litigation, it is difficult to predict outcomes in litigation in exact percentages in contrast to a range of percentages.
- *Hindsight bias.* Parties and counsel invariably overestimate the predictability of past events and fail to recognize, when making predictions, that hindsight is 20/20. As a consequence, the assessment of whether or not conduct is wrongful is likely to be determined differently by one person making an objective decision before the fact and another person (or jury) assessing, after the fact, whether conduct was wrongful and, if so, whether actual damage resulted from alleged wrongful conduct. For example, a decision that it is not necessary to adopt a safety measure will be viewed more critically after the fact, in the context of a trial to determine whether the failure to take the precaution caused actual harm.
- *Reactive devaluation.* Parties and counsel often will discredit information or reject a proposal from an adversary solely because of the fact that it was proposed by the adversary—a phenomenon known as reactive devaluation (see section 5.2.3). (Overall, *attributional bias* is a closely related phenomenon—namely, the tendency of people hostile to an adversary to impute negative intent to the adversary, even in the absence of any negative acts, which makes cooperation difficult.)

Because of the above irrational attachments to positions (or cognitive illusions), it is difficult for parties and counsel to make completely objective assessments about either outcome in litigation or settlement. Settlements are far more rational when parties make an effort to recognize whether any of the above cognitive illusions or biases have influenced their assessments.

A more thorough analysis of the above issues, including studies on principles of cognitive illusions, can be found in chapter 4.

6.8.13 Checklist of Questions for Client

The following is a checklist of questions to review with the client in preparing for a mediation:

- What was the sequence of events, facts?
- What business interests are involved in this dispute?
- How do you feel about this dispute? How does the other side feel about the dispute?
- What do you want/need?
- What is most important?
- What is least important?
- What do you believe are the strengths and weaknesses of your case? What are the worst facts? What are the best facts?
- What do you believe are the strengths and weaknesses of your opponent's case? What are their worst facts? What are their best facts?
- What alternatives would you consider if agreement cannot be reached?
- What is the most attractive alternative?
- What is the least attractive alternative?
- How would you prioritize the alternatives?
- What are your bottom-line monetary recovery needs?
- What are your non-monetary needs?
- What are your settlement expectations?
- What compromises will you consider to reach a negotiated settlement?
- What are you unwilling to compromise under any circumstances?
- What do you believe are the opposing party's interests, goals, and objectives in the dispute?
- Can you prioritize the opposing party's interests?
- What is the opposing party's interest in a negotiated settlement?
- Are you interested in privacy or do you prefer a public forum?
- Are you interested in a speedy resolution?
- Do you have an interest in preserving a continuing relationship with the opposing party?
- Do you have any contracts or relationships with the opposing party that are not the subject of this dispute?
- Will you have to do business with the opposing party in the future?
- What are the barriers to a settlement?
- Do you believe that emotions or hostilities will be a barrier to settlement?

- Who are the decision makers for the other side?
- How would you describe the personalities of the other side's decision makers?
- Are there any other potential parties with an interest, who, if notified, would increase the likelihood of serious negotiations taking place?
- Who should be participating directly in the presentation of the case? The negotiations?
- What particular concerns do you have about mediating this dispute?

6.9 Protect Confidentiality

Confidentiality is a cornerstone of the mediation process. Because of the uneven protection given mediation communications under state and federal law, however, parties are well advised to agree to confidentiality as a matter of contract with and among the mediators and the parties.

Generally, confidentiality is protected to some extent and defined by several sources—evidence codes, statutes, contract, the mediator, and third-party provider rules and procedures. However, since the protections of confidentiality are far from absolute, counsel and business representatives should understand the sometimes-confusing distinction between confidentiality and privilege and take affirmative measures to secure the maximum level of protection for the client.

While Federal Rule of Evidence 408 and many state counterparts may give significant protection for statements made in compromise negotiations, the rules of evidence cover only what is admitted and excluded at trial and are not guarantees of confidentiality. For example, the rule does not bar an adverse party from using a mediation statement in a subsequent deposition. Nor does the rule limit the use of a statement in an arbitration, in the press, or in public.

The "privilege" created by state statutes may provide a much broader scope of protection for statements made during the course of a mediation than federal rules (there is no federal "privilege" for mediation specifically). State statutes also may protect the mediator from being called as a witness in subsequent arbitration or litigation proceedings, and also protect his or her work product from being subpoenaed. The Uniform Mediation Act goes further than many state statutes in protecting mediation statements but has not been adopted in many states. As of this writing, California rules are widely considered to provide the most absolute protection available. States such as New York provide more minimal protection.

Complicated conflicts of law questions can arise when mediation participants come from different states, the case came out of federal court, and the mediation itself is in yet another state.

As a consequence of evidentiary rules and statutory privileges, information presented during a mediation is generally held in confidence by all participants and cannot be deemed discoverable during litigation. However, information that is otherwise admissible or discoverable is not protected merely because of its presentation during mediation. Depending on the jurisdiction, there are also several important exceptions to the confidential nature of mediation, including the legal requirement to disclose certain information, such as the revelation of plans to commit a crime.

Ultimately, in order to further safeguard the confidentiality of the proceedings, counsel should expressly agree **by contract**, with the mediator and among themselves, that all statements made in the mediation are for the purpose of exploring the potential for compromise. These agreements may include the destruction of the mediator's notes at the conclusion of the mediation, and which provide additional protections, such as prohibiting public disclosure of the terms of any settlement agreement. Many mediators will include a provision on confidentiality and provide these additional protections in the mediator's agreement, with the parties setting forth the terms of his or her engagement. Additionally, where the parties are using an ADR provider, the organization will have procedural rules that address the issue of confidentiality.

While the concern for confidentiality is a legitimate one, parties to a dispute need to be practical and recognize that mediation provides a higher level of confidentiality than the most likely alternative—unassisted negotiations between the parties.

6.10 Prepare Draft Settlement Agreement, including Potential Business Term Sheets

Many mediation advocates give little thought in advance of mediation to the issues that need to be addressed in the event of a settlement. Preparing a draft of a binding term sheet in advance of mediation will save valuable time and assure counsel that all key settlement issues will be addressed before the parties adjourn. The exercise of drafting will require the consideration of the usual settlement issues such as releases, confidentiality, non-disparagement, and termination of any pending litigation. This exercise will also permit counsel to create a checklist of any specific issues that need to be addressed in a settlement agreement. Counsel should also consider the advisability of arbitrating any future disputes that may arise between the parties.

In addition, if non-monetary terms are part of the settlement, it makes tremendous sense for counsel to draft language they anticipate might be part of the mediated agreement, such as modifications to existing agreements.

During the mediation, particularly if a settlement involves multiple parts, it is a good idea to request that the parties involved prepare written offers and present the offers themselves in joint sessions so that the terms are clear and the parties have a chance to ask questions before caucusing about the response.

Chapter 7
Representing the Client in the Mediation

7.1 Counsel's Role in Mediation Sessions

The role of counsel in the mediation sessions themselves will vary depending on the counsel's background and function and the procedural posture of the dispute. As noted, depending on the potential outcomes of the mediation, it may be that a transactional counsel from an outside firm will play a leading role; alternatively, a corporate litigation or transactional inside counsel may perform the primary counsel function without outside counsel involved. Outside counsel litigators may also be in the lead, particularly when a mediation occurs well into a litigation or arbitration process.

Whatever the background of the lawyer, she has a continuing role as advocate, negotiator, counselor, and problem-solver. Because a mediator often will involve the representatives of a party directly from the outset of the mediation session, some attorneys assume a passive role and are almost non-participants in the process. At the other extreme, some attorneys—often from a litigation background and locked in a litigation mindset—argue their clients' positions relentlessly and lose opportunities to advance their clients' interests by failing to take a more collaborative approach to the negotiations or to permit the client representative to be actively involved in the process.

Throughout the mediation, counsel should continue to pursue with the client the negotiating strategy adopted at the preparation stage. Counsel should remain an advocate in constant pursuit of the client's interests and goals. At the same time, counsel should listen carefully to the mediator, the opposing party and opposing counsel. The mediation sessions offer a time to learn more about the other party's position in the dispute and an opportunity to reevaluate the client's goals and strategies. These sessions also offer a meaningful opportunity to solve the client's problem and accomplish its objectives.

7.2 Opening Statement

As previously noted, many experienced counsel and mediators have come to the conclusion that the risk that making a legal "opening statement" setting forth their position and attempting to convince the other side will get the initial mediation session off to a very bad start by inflaming the situation and is not worth any conceivable benefit, especially when there are substitutes (such as exchanging statements in advance of the mediation) that may achieve the laudable goals of an opening statement without the risks. Even a more business-focused client presentation can go off the rails if not carefully managed. As noted in the discussion of common barriers to resolution, the repetition of one's position or posture can serve to reinforce one's belief in that position.

A robust preparation process of the type we advocate in this book will provide opportunities for the parties to present their views in advance of the live meetings but avoid what can become an inherently adversarial live presentation.

Encouraging business representatives to say a few opening words in support of the process of negotiation and compromise, without getting into the weeds of the dispute, however, is always advisable.

However, in considering how to proceed, counsel and the business should consider that an opening statement in a joint session presents an opportunity for the client to tell its story, live, directly to the other party, after what may have been a long period of business silence, and ask themselves, and the mediator, whether or not this opportunity is so important to the client that the risks of such direct communication first thing at the mediation should be assumed. If the matter is already in litigation, and regardless of whether or not the story is presented by counsel or a representative of the client, the presenter should focus on what a court will hear, not on what happened. Recognizing that the mediation session may in this structure move from a form of mini-trial to a pure negotiation, counsel should lay a foundation for the negotiating positions the client ultimately will pursue. While it is appropriate to show anger or other feelings about the dispute, an opening statement should not use emotionally charged words that might simply antagonize the other side. To maximize the likelihood of success in mediation, counsel should demonstrate confidence in its position and, at the same time, indicate a willingness to engage in a good-faith exploration of possible resolution.

Finally, counsel and representatives of the parties should direct their comments to the other side, not to the mediator. It is the other side that needs to be persuaded.

Ultimately, whether or not to have opening legal or business statements is not a one-size-fits-all assessment and should be discussed with the mediator. The "disappearing joint session" phenomenon discussed by practitioners (which really means the disappearing legal opening statement) is in part a result of more experience with the process over the years and recognition of the importance of preparation. It is also important to acknowledge that a skilled mediator often will have joint sessions in addition to the "opening" joint meeting, of the full group or smaller functional meetings, which will enable clients to share their thoughts during the course of the proceedings.

7.3 Use Mediator to Facilitate Negotiations

Counsel should recognize the competing tensions that exist in the relationship between counsel and the mediator. In a mediation, the parties are not only negotiating with each other, but the parties and counsel are also engaged in a mini-negotiation with the mediator, at least at the outset of the process. At the same time, by trusting the mediator with sensitive information about resolution, the parties are likely to enhance the potential for a successful resolution. Parties and counsel should also not hesitate to ask the mediator for needed information, make suggestions regarding process (such as asking for a business executive–only or an inside counsel–only meeting), ask the mediator to present a proposal as his or her own in order to overcome reactive devaluation, or ask the mediator for substantive suggestions on settlement.

7.4 Keys to Effective Negotiations

As described in section 1.3, the process of mediation is one of facilitated negotiations. Success in mediation, therefore, very much depends on the negotiating skill of the participants. On the whole, even highly experienced lawyers and business executives approach negotiations on somewhat of an intuitive basis. Yet, studies on negotiations establish that negotiation skills can be learned, and that the skilled negotiator will outperform the average negotiator by substantial margins. While the process of negotiations is itself the subject of numerous books and articles, the following sections offer some of the principal keys to successful negotiations in a mediation setting.

7.4.1 Ask Questions

Studies on negotiation demonstrate that skilled negotiators spend more than twice as much time gathering information as a percentage of their negotiating behavior as do average negotiators. By asking questions, testing for understanding, and summarizing, the skilled negotiator is in a far better position to understand the other side's interests, issues, perceptions, and settlement positions.

7.4.2 Listen Carefully and Actively

Information is power. A skilled negotiator will listen to every word to learn more about the other side's positions, perceptions, and interests and to discern signals that may reveal the other side's settlement position. For example, the statement "We're not prepared to make a significant move" should generate the responsive question "What do you regard as *significant*?" or "What move *are* you prepared to make?" All too frequently, counsel will lose an opportunity to advance the negotiations by missing the subtle cues that can be learned from the spoken words, tone, and nonverbal conduct of the participants in a negotiation. They may be making judgements about what they are hearing, preparing a rebuttal, or interrupting instead of truly focusing on what is being said. While we all know how to listen, it is critical in a negotiation to filter out all the internal voices that may distract us from our full attention. Many of the suggestions in this section and immediately above are described by some practitioners as engaging in *active listening*.

7.4.3 Develop Negotiating Power

Only two years after co-authoring *Getting to Yes: Negotiating Agreement Without Giving In,*[18] Roger Fisher recognized that this seminal work on using mediation to develop win-win solutions devoted insufficient attention to the issue of power. In his article "Negotiating Power," Fisher explores the potential for successful negotiations as the result of recognizing and developing the sources of "real negotiating power."[19] While it is a common misperception that real power arises from raw power or a tough approach to negotiations, Fisher described the following six kinds of power that, when properly understood and utilized, have a substantial ability to influence the outcome of a negotiation.

- *The power of skill and knowledge.* As suggested above, negotiating skills can be learned and a skilled negotiator can out perform the average negotiator by substantial margins. Moreover, the more information a party learns about the facts, the rights, the interests, and the people involved, the greater one's negotiating position.
- *The power of a good relationship.* A person's capacity to exert influence is substantially enhanced if he or she has established a well-deserved reputation for candor and integrity. Given the fact that the process of negotiations is one of communication, the process will be significantly enhanced by a good relationship with the other side. Not only will the other side listen better to messages delivered, but they will be more

18. FISHER, *supra* note 9.
19. Roger Fisher, *Negotiating Power*, 27 AM BEHAV SCI 149 (1983).

likely to be open when giving messages in response. These messages may well include signals that reveal the other side's settlement position.

- *The power of a good alternative to negotiation.* Power in negotiation very much depends on how well a party will do in the event negotiations fail. For example, a customer complaining that a supplier has breached a supply agreement by failing to make timely deliveries will have substantial bargaining power if it can develop a readily available second source should the negotiations fail.
- *The power of an elegant solution.* The likelihood of success in negotiations can be enhanced by developing as many options as possible, especially a creative option that works well for both parties.
- *The power of legitimacy (fairness).* A party's negotiating power can be substantially enhanced by developing a set of standards (legal precedent, industry standards or policy considerations) that demonstrate the legitimacy (or fairness) of any proposal made to the other side.
- *The power of commitment.* A skilled negotiator will formulate an offer in ways that maximize the cumulative impact of each of the above sources of power. If an affirmative commitment to such an offer is rejected, a negative commitment (a threat or statement that no agreement is acceptable), may possibly undermine the potential for a successful result. As a consequence, it is generally unwise to make any such negative commitment until one has made the most of all of the other elements of negotiating power.

7.4.4 Understand Principles of Leverage

While one party in negotiations may have greater power in absolute (or objective) terms, the advantages of leverage can be determined by inquiring whether one of the parties to a dispute has a situational advantage. In many instances, the party with less power may have greater leverage. For example, a patent infringement claim by an inventor against a Fortune 500 company might represent just another claim in normal times. However, the same claim might present a strategic problem for the company if it is about to be acquired. In such a circumstance, while the large company has greater power, the inventor might have significant leverage in any negotiation to resolve the dispute. Global supply disruptions caused by pandemics can also give leverage to smaller players. Leverage can be assessed by determining, for example, which party controls the status quo, whether time is an advantage for either party, or whether one party has a greater need for confidentiality.

7.4.5 Demands and Offers

Demands and offers generally will be regarded by an adverse party as falling into one of the zones illustrated by Figure 7.1.

In deciding what initial offer to make, the negotiator should recognize that any offer considered an insult may not generate any response and may possibly disrupt the negotiation. Conversely, opening with too much may embolden the other side and make the bargaining process harder, not easier. Further, there is always the potential that too large a move may exceed the bottom-line requirements of the other side.

By making the first credible offer, parties have an opportunity to anchor the negotiation and adjust the expectations of the other side. In making an offer at the extreme edge of the credible zone, parties should advance a rationale to support the offer or expressly suggest that the offer is negotiable.

Once the negotiations are underway, counsel and parties in a mediation should consider empowering the mediator to control the flow of the negotiations. After having met with all parties in caucus sessions, the mediator can offer suggestions on process, comment on proposed offers and demands (including observations as to whether a next step may be perceived as violating negotiation norms such as the need for subsequent offers always improving upon previous ones, transparency in changes to offers and the need for reciprocity), especially if the mediator considers a negotiating move to be too large or too small. Especially with regard to the pace of the negotiations, parties need to trust the mediator and recognize that it may be counterproductive to try to close too fast. Of course, while the mediator may be in the best position to offer suggestions to advance the process, the dispute belongs to the parties—not to the mediator. Ultimately, the parties must decide what proposals to make and whether or not an amicable resolution presents a more attractive alternative than the consequences of failing to settle.

<table>
<tr><td colspan="3">Claimant</td><td></td><td></td></tr>
<tr><td>Insult</td><td>Credible</td><td>Reasonable</td><td>Credible</td><td>Insult</td></tr>
<tr><td></td><td></td><td colspan="3">Respondent</td></tr>
</table>

Figure 7.1 Zones of Demands and Offers

7.4.6 Track the Negotiations; Present the Offers

In direct business negotiations, parties would never dream of leaving the presentation of their term sheet to a third party. Too often, parties assume it is up to the mediator to keep track of and write up proposals and present them to the other side without considering whether or not this is appropriate, effective or presents risks.

We often ask the parties to generate written proposals that can be discussed as a team, particularly if there is anything more than money involved in the proposed settlement. In the first instance, this permits the negotiating team to ensure internal agreement on the terms and may raise gaps for consideration by the team that need to be addressed. The parties can also present the proposals to each other, with coaching on the appropriate messages to accompany the offers. This permits the receiving party to ask questions and keeps the mediation feeling like a negotiation—and ensures that the proposal is presented as the party would like it to be.

In any event, each side, counsel and client, should chart the progress of the negotiations by keeping a record of each new offer, demand or proposal. One way to do this is to maintain a joint record of the proposals in one document (offer A, offer B, etc.) After the first several moves in a negotiation, a pattern may emerge from the proportional moves made by the parties. By reviewing the movement of the parties and the remaining gap, counsel can better determine whether smaller or larger moves should be made to advance the negotiations and accomplish the goals of the client.

7.4.7 Use Demonstrative Aids

Selective use of charts, exhibits and other visual aids can be very persuasive in mediation. In a joint session, an exhibit setting forth a chronology of a business dispute, illustrating a design defect or a chart offering an accounting of probable damages can offer the other side a glimpse of what a jury is likely to see at trial. Moreover, unlike at trial, where an exhibit is marked and shown to the jury for a limited period of time, a visual aid can make a meaningful impact by remaining in the mediation room for an extended period of time. To the extent correspondence, memos or other documents are available to contradict positions likely to be taken by the adverse party, they should be available, ideally exchanged before the mediation but certainly available in mediation to be shared with the mediator.

7.5 Encourage Client and Non-Litigator Participation

As we have discussed, many mediation advocates are litigators who, as a consequence of their training and experience, often find it difficult to cede control of the process to the client or otherwise rid themselves of a "litigation mindset." Once again, it is important to stress that the client needs to tell its story and have its "day in court." More importantly, business executives and inside counsel have the best understanding of the company's interests and objectives and often are in a better position than counsel to suggest or accept business-driven solutions to a dispute, or negotiate the terms, as this is what they do every day. Similarly, litigators should consider whether or not their non-litigator, transactional colleagues may be able to make a contribution.

7.6 Solve the Problem

By taking a problem-solving approach to a dispute, counsel and the parties have the potential to create solutions that work for both parties. Much has been written about the potential for "win-win" solutions. While the potential is very real, it requires the participant in a negotiation to think "out of the box"—to continually brainstorm for creative solutions in meetings between counsel and the client, in joint sessions with the other sides, and in caucus sessions with the mediator. The downtime that occurs when a mediator is meeting with other parties in caucus sessions presents a particularly good time for party representatives to engage in such a brainstorming exercise. Counsel can enhance the potential for a creative solution by mining the depths of the parties' interests and by taking a collaborative approach to the negotiations. Ultimately, the parties may identify new opportunities such as, for example, amending the terms of a contract unrelated to the dispute or acquiring some or all of the assets (or shares) of the other party.

7.7 Counsel's Role at End of Mediation Sessions

Whether or not the mediation sessions produce an agreement, counsel should be mindful of his or her continuing role as counselor and advocate. Any settlement should be memorialized in a binding term sheet and signed by the parties to avoid any possible remorse by one of the parties or any later disagreement concerning the terms of settlement. If there is an agreement, counsel should make certain that any written agreement provides full protection for all of the client's concerns. If an agreement is not reached, counsel should immediately meet with the client to explore alternative negotiation and litigation strategies. If the client's interests are likely to be enhanced by the mediator's continuing involvement, counsel may want to initiate and help structure the mediator's continuing role.

7.8 Ethical Standards for Lawyers in Mediation

The rules of professional conduct generally will govern a lawyer's conduct in a mediation setting. Most states have enacted codes that follow the ABA Model Rules of Professional Conduct. Since a mediation is primarily a negotiation, a lawyer will be expected in a mediation to adhere to the same standards as in an unassisted negotiation. The most important ethical rules are those governing advocacy, truthfulness, confidentiality, and advice to the client. In particular, a lawyer has a duty to keep a client reasonably informed about the status of a matter and to promptly reply to reasonable requests for information from the client. This duty would require a lawyer, among other things, to advise a client about any settlement offer made during the course of a mediation. Further, counsel should be mindful throughout the course of negotiations and in the mediation session of the requirements of Rule 4.1 of the ABA Model Rules of Professional Conduct concerning "Truthfulness in Statements to Others." Rule 4.1, among other things, states that counsel shall not, in the course of representing a client, knowingly make a false statement of material fact or law to a third person.[20]

7.9 10 Practice Tips for Joint Sessions

Below is a summary of major points for the advocates in mediation joint sessions:

1. Confirm participation in good faith.
2. Consider whether to use opening statements or whether pre-mediation communications can substitute and reduce tensions or whether points can be made during the mediation at times other than the beginning. If necessary, opening statements can assist to tell client's story, educate the mediator, and persuade the other side, but many practitioners believe that the risk of getting the mediation off to a bad start outweighs the benefits.
3. Discuss what a court will hear, not what happened.
4. Direct communications to the other side, not to the mediator.

20. See https://www.americanbar.org/groups/professional_responsibility/publications/model_rules_of_professional_conduct/model_rules_of_professional_conduct_table_of_contents/.

5. Consider client participation and non-litigator legal participation.
6. Help the mediator clarify the disputed issues.
7. Permit venting, but do not antagonize.
8. Do not review the history of prior negotiations.
9. Use visual aids.
10. Listen actively and ask questions.

7.10 10 Practice Tips for Caucus Sessions

Below is a summary of major points for the advocate in mediation caucus sessions:

1. Confirm the mediator's pledge of confidentiality.
2. Encourage client participation.
3. Make proposals to generate movement; do not overreact to undesirable proposals. The best antidote to an unacceptable offer is to make a counteroffer.
4. Decide how best to convey offers for accuracy and negotiation flow—through the mediator, through the parties, or both.
5. Ask the mediator to recommend substantive proposals.
6. Make process suggestions to the mediator.
7. Track (chart) all negotiating positions during mediation.
8. When the mediator meets with the other side, use the time to reevaluate positions and to brainstorm.
9. Listen actively; information is power.
10. Be patient; the process takes time.

7.11 25 Practice Tips for Effective Mediation Advocacy

The following practice tips are offered to assist counsel with their preparation for a mediation:

1. Before selecting a mediator, carefully examine the mediator's reputation, expertise, personality, style, and experience.
2. Interview mediator candidates to assess their experience, style, and qualifications.
3. Participate in the design of the mediation process.
4. View mediation as a process that includes robust information exchange and other preparation before any joint live mediation sessions and be prepared to invest in that process in order to improve chances of success and preparation for any ensuing litigation or arbitration.

5. Be certain that all necessary parties and decision makers will be present during the mediation, or work with stakeholders internally to ensure alignment and, as necessary, availability.
6. Make sure that representatives of adverse parties have comparable settlement authority.
7. Set aside sufficient time for the process.
8. Before the mediation, perform a cost–benefit and litigation risk analysis.
9. Avoid irrational attachments to positions.
10. Review with your client their interests, goals, objectives, and business needs. Prioritize the needs of your client and the opposing party.
11. Develop your client's BATNA and WATNA.
12. Educate your client about the mediation process; explain the roles of the mediator, the advocate, and the client; and encourage investment in preparation for the best chance of success.
13. Prepare for persuasive negotiations, not litigation.
14. Assess your client's ability to be articulate and determine in advance the most effective level of client participation.
15. Prepare client representatives for the likelihood that a mediator will ask questions such as, "How do you feel about the dispute?" and "What is most important to you?"
16. Develop a specific negotiating strategy for the mediation. Continually reassess your strategy and revise it, as appropriate.
17. Prepare a concise opening statement that includes a factual summary and outline of the relevant issues and the strengths of your client's legal positions. Share this with the other party before the mediation or at appropriate points during the live sessions if that will not unproductively inflame tensions, or simply use it as a guide to ensure that the mediator and the other party understand your key point.
18. Direct any argument to the opposing parties, not to counsel or the mediator.
19. Avoid the use of emotionally charged language. When appropriate, express empathy for the other parties' concerns.
20. Listen carefully. Parties are more open in a mediation session than in unassisted negotiations. Be on the lookout for signals from opposing parties throughout the mediation process.
21. Prepare in advance a few good reasons why the other party should move toward your settlement proposal.

22. Develop creative proposals that take into account underlying business interests and relationships between the parties.
23. Ask the mediator, where appropriate, to present settlement options as his or her own idea in order to avoid reactive devaluation.
24. Decide in advance what steps you and your client will take if mediation fails to achieve a negotiated settlement. Anticipate the measures likely to be taken by adverse parties if the dispute is not resolved.
25. Remember that a "failed" mediation may be the catalyst for a subsequent negotiated resolution of the dispute.

Chapter 8
The Business Executive's Roles in Mediation

8.1 The Business Executive's Roles in Mediation

Throughout this book, we have made it clear that in commercial mediation, the roles of the non-lawyer business person, as well as the company's inside counsel, are critical. Business executives in the mediation need to take ownership of the entire process and result, even if litigation or arbitration has commenced. They should ask to be educated by their legal departments or lawyers about the various dispute prevention and resolution options. They also should understand the value of investing in a robust mediation process that includes extensive preparation in order to avoid protracted time and expense in resolving disputes using an adjudicative process.

8.2 11 Practice Tips for Business Executives in Mediation

Here are 11 practice tips for effective business executive participation in a commercial mediation, which also apply to inside counsel when they are considered the client by the outside firm participating in the mediation:

1. Invest your time and your company's money in a robust mediation process, including information exchange and other preparation for live sessions.
2. Understand and explain to counsel the cause of the dispute, including any personal issues or technical difficulties, and share thoughts on negotiating leverage.
3. Work with stakeholders in your company to ensure alignment with business objectives and goals.
4. Ensure that business participants include not only those who were involved in the dispute but "higher up" executives with a more objective perspective, as well as functions such as finance and tax as appropriate.
5. Work with counsel and the mediator to assess the role of counsel, the business participants, and the mediator, and be prepared to play a leading role through negotiation, generation of spreadsheets, etc.
6. Get adequate settlement authority or have the business person with authority at the mediation or efficiently available via virtual means.
7. Work to develop non-monetary business solutions or reworkings of failed agreements based upon your assessment of the root causes of the dispute.
8. Insist on a detailed explanation from counsel of the cost and disruption of a litigation or arbitration of the dispute, and an objective assessment of litigation risk.
9. Be prepared to speak to the mediator without counsel present.
10. Try to understand the other side's business needs and perspective and see if these can be met consistent with your needs and interests.
11. Do not overreact to an unacceptable offer; instead, be patient and make a counteroffer to generate movement.

Chapter 9
Special Topics in Commercial Mediation

9.1 Introduction

Certain types of commercial mediations present special issues beyond what has been considered "typical" in earlier chapters. In this chapter, we address *deal mediation*, an early form of mediation in which a mediator is directly involved in the negotiation of a contract, the retention of a neutral before any dispute has developed in connection with a transaction (standing and standby mediators), and co-mediations; take a systematic look at the issues presented by mediations involving multiple parties; say a few words about class action mediations since businesses often find themselves involved in these types of litigations; identify key issues if an insurer will be playing a role in the mediation; and finally, discuss topics relating to mediation of intellectual property disputes.

9.2 Deal Mediation

In deal mediation, direct negotiators solicit the assistance of a neutral third-party mediator in structuring and negotiating a business arrangement from the beginning. An effective deal mediator is likely a transactional or subject matter expert with significant experience in negotiation of business deals. There are tremendous advantages that can be gained from having a neutral help the parties focus on the types of issues that Roger Fisher and William Ury identify as key to win-win negotiations: separating people from problems, focusing on interest, not positions, inventing options for mutual gain, and, very importantly, using objective criteria. All of the mediator functions and skills outlined elsewhere in this book (reframing issues, setting the agenda, etc.) can be very productive in this setting with the right mediator, and we think that this type of mediation is underutilized.

Although a contract "dispute" has not arisen as the contract has not yet been signed, deal mediators may be particularly useful if the parties expect that negotiations may be challenging. For example, one of us mediated a patent license required by the terms of a litigation settlement agreement only if and when a patent was issued by the relevant patent office. Issuance of the patent triggered an expedited license negotiation. The negotiation required a joint assessment of the strength of a number of patents and potential business terms beyond the license in order to bridge valuation gaps. Business principles led the negotiations with the assistance and suggestions of the mediator. The settlement agreement called for a "facilitator," but the parties agreed that mediation was the more appropriate characterization of the process.

9.3 Standing/Standby Neutral Mediation and Mediation Windows

Mediators can be retained to assist in the resolution of disputes that arise in the course of a business arrangement before any disputes arise. For example, in one health care joint venture, the parties retained a "standing" mediator to become familiar with the terms and objectives of the joint venture and be ready to assist in the resolution of disputes. This is somewhat similar to, although different from, a useful self-help tool, the retention by both sides of a "relationship" or "alliance" manager. Relationship or alliance managers are acknowledged non-neutral employees of a business; nevertheless, it is an alliance manager's role to help resolve disputes and work to improve communications (and some alliance managers take mediation training courses to improve their skills). The added neutrality and objective position of a mediator can be helpful in the resolution of disputes and reframing communications. (And alliance managers should note that mediation training would be a very good additional tool for their toolbox.)

Once a litigation or arbitration has been filed, parties can agree on a mediator in advance who can step in at an appropriate point—this can make the transition to mediation easier and less a sign of perceived weakness since it has already been agreed (a standby mediator). This eases the transition to mediation and concerns that a suggestion that the parties mediate will be considered a sign of weakness. Going further, a mediator can be retained to follow along with the dispute and make suggestions regarding potentially productive inflection points to conduct mediation discussions or step in at an agreed time—a standing mediator. The concept of "settlement counsel," a lawyer retained by a party not to be a direct part of the litigation team, but rather following the litigation and looking for settlement opportunities, is similar. Like an alliance manager, however, settlement counsel are generally retained by one party to represent their interests. The mediator is retained by both parties and plays a neutral role.

Relatedly, we are increasingly seeing business parties agree to schedule a mediation window during the course of an arbitration, and some arbitrators suggest this as part of their scheduling orders. The window requires that the parties mediate at a particular point in time, or that mediation is at least considered. This is a very useful technique, which removes concerns about the appearance of weakness and can get the parties talking.

9.4 Success in Mediation Before an Arbitration or Litigation is Filed

We have noted the advantages of avoiding the inevitable escalation and exacerbation of a conflict by attempting to mediate before filing a litigation or arbitration. What steps should parties take to ensure success?

Throughout this book, we have emphasized the importance of putting aside a litigation mindset, serious business involvement, and a significant investment in preparation. In a pre-litigation or arbitration situation, we say, even more so on all counts, buttressed by a degree of transparency with the mediator and the other side that may seem uncomfortable, but which is critical to resolving the dispute at this early stage.

Parties should consider trying to develop a business negotiation look and feel to the mediation by having business participants and inside counsel assume lead roles and, as we have remarked in earlier chapters, acknowledge explicitly that the conversation proceeds on two tracks: looking for a business solution and assessing legal risk.

The mediation process should be used to substitute for the lack of a complaint and answer and discovery by having the parties voluntarily share information about key topics and their contentions in exchanged position papers so that the live meetings are not taken up with the mediator explaining these topics to each side—and the parties are prepared to evaluate their positions. The entire mediation process will need to be more flexible as the parties learn the facts, often at the same time as the mediator.

The preparation process can and should be quite robust. We have each engaged in preparation processes that took two or more months and involved numerous exchanges of information, including chronologies, charts, technical information, and other materials—and even the retention of a joint expert to resolve an issue about whether or not a pharmaceutical relied upon certain proprietary know-how.

At one extreme, one of us participated in day-long witness interviews alongside outside counsel also learning the facts and documents (which were collected during the interviews) for the first time as the parties strove to avoid the litigation of a long-term collaboration. This helped develop the facts in an objective way through real-time reality testing. This process was suggested by the lawyers themselves at the behest of their clients.

This sharing, transparency, and flexibility, potentially involving little or no opportunity to preview and prepare clients, does not come naturally to a litigator charged with controlling processes and shaping or withholding information. In the right matters and with the right mediator, however, it will help clients get back to business without stepping into an adjudicated process that may well serve only to exacerbate conflict and quickly spiral out of their direct control.

9.5 Co-Mediation

Co-mediation involving more than one (usually two) mediators often is used in training to help less experienced mediators benefit from the experience of more advanced practitioners. But there are many good reasons to consider this beyond the training context, although there clearly will need to be a transparent discussion about (1) the total cost of the mediators' combined services, and (2) the mediators' respective roles and responsibilities.

Using two mediators can be helpful for the following reasons:

1. Enables the mediators to pick up on nonverbal cues and signaling better than a single mediator can.
2. Permits an expert in a field to work with a mediation process expert.
3. Allows mediators to divide up issues on a complex matter, for example by running simultaneous caucus sessions on different topics or with different parties (see section 9.6).
4. Gives mediators an opportunity to have mediator caucuses to compare what they are hearing and discuss strategies and next steps—"two heads are better than one."
5. Permits a mediator knowledgeable in the language and culture of one or both parties to team with a mediator who has different expertise.
6. Gives the parties comfort that they will have two neutrals to "convince" of their positions.

Some of the concerns about co-mediation, which can be ameliorated by communication and practice between the co-mediators and attention to blended rates in terms of fees, are as follows:

1. Can increase cost.
2. Are co-mediators equal? Is one the junior? Is one an expert?
3. Incorporate sharing of information that each gains in private caucuses or otherwise; asymmetry of information received can be a challenge.
4. Confusion among roles.
5. Clashes in style.

9.6 Multiple Parties

Multiple-party disputes are common in commercial settings and in settings that confront businesses quite often in the United States, even though they technically involve consumers. Common multiparty disputes include:

- Class actions (see section 9.7)
- Mass torts
- Construction
- Environmental/land use
- Insurance coverage
- Complex, commercial disputes
- Public sector disputes

Multiparty disputes are not necessarily more difficult to resolve than two-party disputes. For example, disputes with multiple corporate defendants often are less difficult than disputes between two business partners who, after long-term business and personal relationship, are litigating claims of breach of fiduciary duties. In addition, multi-party disputes do not necessarily involve multilateral negotiations, as some defense groups are highly organized, have a representative negotiating team, have decided all allocation issues, and speak with one voice.

In multi-party disputes, we also look to some of the same barriers to resolution we have explored in connection with two-party disputes, such as:

- Emotions
- Communication
- Asymmetries of information
- Uneven focus
- Divergent predictions of BATNA
- Issues between client and litigation counsel (reporting, fees, etc.)
- Failure to recognize and exchange information about interests
- Lack of creativity
- Selective perception and advocacy bias
- Other cognitive illusions and irrational attachment to positions

Nevertheless, multi-party mediations do present special challenges and opportunities. These issues are addressed in the checklist form below.

9.6.1 Distribution of Common Barriers to Resolution

The common barriers to resolution discussed above are not necessarily evenly distributed:

- Some plaintiffs' (or defense) groups may be highly emotional, others not at all. Each requires different mediator approaches.
- Some parties will have done "merits homework" on liability and damages—legal research, expert consultation—others not at all.
- Some parties will have involved decision makers, insurers, etc., others not at all.
- Greater numbers provide places to "hide."
- Group leaders may have been formally chosen, externally imposed, or naturally (officially/unofficially) "emerged."
- Conflicting interests across the *v.* and/or within each "side" may prevent emergence of a leader.
- Results may be disorganization—incoherence, lack of a plan, or inability to define goals, let alone achieve them.

9.6.2 Preparation Is Even More Important Than in a Two-Party Dispute

Although we have consistently emphasized the value of looking at mediation as a process that includes preparation, live sessions, and follow-through for any mediation, in a multiparty situation, fairly extensive preparation is even more important.

1. The mediator should work with counsel and parties well in advance of mediation through exchanged statements, confidential submissions, and private meetings to identify key issues of process and begin to plan a roadmap for resolution.
2. Attention will need to be focused on the alignment of parties:
   - Are some defendants indemnified by plaintiffs? If so, should they be placed in caucus rooms with plaintiffs or separate caucus rooms?
   - Are defendants still pursuing their crossclaims? Or have they entered into a joint defense?

3. The mediator will need to work with counsel to identify the negotiating groups.
   - How organized are the plaintiffs? Defendants? Is there a formal "steering committee" or negotiating team?
   - Who comprises the negotiating team?
   - What role will each team member play?
   - Who are the real leaders on the negotiating team?
   - Who are the "destabilizers" on the negotiating team?
   - Who will participate in caucus sessions with the mediator? The entire assembled group? Or a small representative team?
4. Identify the agendas of each party and negotiating team.
   - Recognize who are the "moderates"—those who are flexible, who express a willingness to consider a number of options, and who recognize the legitimacy of the needs of other parties.
   - Recognize who are the "extremists"—those who rigidly hold onto a minority position and continually direct the agenda to serve their own, narrow interests.
5. Begin to develop structure and process for the negotiations.
6. Explore potential for use of experts.
7. Review with counsel the identity of all participants to assure that the right people are in the room and that decision makers have appropriate authority.
8. Make sure that the facilities will be adequate (some multiparty mediations require several conference rooms, and some require auditorium-size rooms), and explore the advantages of virtual or hybrid mediation in accommodating different groups.

9.6.3 Process Is More Important

- Process buy-in by all participants is critical—have a joint planning call.
- What does everyone need to see and hear?
- Process must be designed to address all barriers, as necessary.
- Confidential submissions are more important; consider asking parties to address the following:
  - A brief description of the business of your client and the roles of party representatives who will be attending the mediation
  - The current posture of the case (pre-litigation? in litigation? arbitration?)

  - Legal positions (rights analysis), including any rebuttal position (including a candid assessment of all parties' principal strengths and weaknesses)
- Probable outcomes (in appellate review or in any subsequent litigation, if this dispute is not resolved in mediation).
- Interests-analysis (issues such as timing, need for confidentiality, linkage to any unrelated issue or dispute, strategic issues, personal relationship issues, need for privacy, internal company issues, impact upon future, etc.).
  - From plaintiffs' perspectives
  - From defense perspectives
  - From each sub-group's perspective
- History of any negotiations (or any discussions touching upon subject of resolution).
- Any suggestions concerning process (including any particular approach the mediator should take).
- Any suggestions concerning possible substantive resolution of dispute (especially any creative solution based upon underlying interests or relationships).
- Factors that may favor resolution.
- Factors that present potential barriers to resolution.
- Estimate of fees and costs in litigation (or arbitration) through conclusion of dispute (if dispute not resolved at mediation).
- What do you believe the other party really wants? What might they find acceptable?
- Process for joint sessions should be established in advance; joint session offers an opportunity to set a tone, exchange views, and use mediator's opening statement to suggest the benchmark for a responsible settlement decision—comparing what can be accomplished in mediation with the parties' "real-world alternative" (not what they may want or need); also opportunity to have each party assess risk (even more important in multiple-party disputes where participants often have had less reporting).
- Should all plaintiffs/defendants be together in one mediation? Or should there be multiple mediations?
- Especially in public sector disputes, the key to success is to identify all stakeholders and to have them participate in the design of the process.

9.6.4 Leadership Is More Important

- Many multiparty plaintiffs and multiparty defendants are extremely disorganized, especially in the initial stages of a dispute—mediator must be more active and provide for greater leadership.
- Realistic time and people management plans are often required (participants need to understand reasons for time constraints).
- Set realistic expectations. Many multiparty mediations require multiple sessions, both *ex parte* and joint.
- Parties will get frustrated . . . let them know it's a part of the process and they need to continue their commitment.
- Always keep the process moving.
- Greater need to take charge and propose solutions.

9.6.5 Evaluation and Assessment of Percentage Allocation

Allocation of damages among defendants often is the most difficult problem.

- Determine in advance of mediation whether there is an agreed-upon allocation plan among defendants.
- If not, begin to develop a process in advance of mediation.
- In multi-defendant mediations, it is not uncommon for defendants to agree upon a target damage number but disagree among and between each other on percentage allocation.
- "It's not our fault, it's their fault."
- Need for consensus that finger-pointing will only increase exposure to plaintiffs—defendants often will set aside crossclaims until a second round of ADR.
- Once a consensus has been reached on a global number, consider a voting procedure that allocates 100 percent points of liability to all defendants except the party voting.
- Such procedure requires a level of transparency and agreement—but procedure usually works (most parties will see similar percentages for all parties once they take their own share out of the equation).
- As an alternative, defendants can each reach tentative agreement to allocate share pending future expedited arbitrations to reallocate.
- Need to recognize and manage issues of partial versus global settlement.
- Need to be more directive, less facilitative (e.g., suggested target offer/suggested allocations).

- Key often is getting parties to back off "principle" arguments, i.e., "we won't pay more than 50 percent of what defendant X pays," and getting parties to recognize that it is the real numbers that count.

Allocation Issues among Plaintiffs

- Many issues are similar to those listed above.
- Most defendants prefer to deal with all plaintiffs in the aggregate.
- Defense offers may possibly be conditioned upon resolution of all claims.
- Some plaintiffs' counsel have little control over their group and will require assistance in developing structures for allocation and distribution.

9.7 Class Actions

Class actions are one form of multi-party mediation. The issues flagged above apply, but special considerations arise in the class action context that deserve special focus. While business-to-business disputes are not often adjudicated in a class action context, they sometimes are, as in healthcare payor–provider or antitrust cases, and certainly, businesses face class action challenges in general from consumers (such as data privacy breaches or product liability) and investors (securities class actions). A quick summary of key issues are listed below given the frequency with which businesses face this type of procedural challenge in the United States.[21]

- These matters often are complex, involving high dollar–value claims, extensive litigation history, complicated data, and, of course, multiple stakeholders. Mediation can be very effective and save immense time and money, but it requires tremendous preparation and organization, like any multiple-party case.

---

21. Many of the issues identified below were discussed in a January 25, 2021, Boston Bar Association CLE program moderated by Conna A. Weiner, "Best Practices in Class Action Mediation: What Advocates Need to Know," with very experienced panelists Eric D. Green of Resolutions, LLC, Patrick Sheehan of Whatley Kallas, and Don Frederico of Pierce Atwood. Eric Green contributed an excellent chapter, *Mega-Disputes and Class Actions*, *in* MEDIATING LEGAL DISPUTES: EFFECTIVE STRATEGIES FOR NEUTRALS AND ADVOCATES 123-144 (Dwight Golann, 2009). Don Frederico has an award-winning blog on class action mediation and settlement issues: https://www.classactionsettlementsandmediation.com. Patrick Sheehan is a widely respected healthcare law practitioner with a national practice.

- A key inflection point is class certification. Strategizing about whether to mediate before a class is certified or after is important for both sides.
  - Are there subclasses that should be treated differently?
  - Class action resolutions often involve more than mere dollars and can include agreements about changes to business practices going forward.
- It is absolutely essential to bear in mind throughout that the settlement—from a process and substance perspective—will have to be approved by a presiding court as "fair, reasonable, and adequate."[22]
  - Focusing on this inevitable fact can help drive agreements.
  - The involvement of a neutral mediator in the structuring of the settlement can give credibility to the result, a fact acknowledged in some court opinions. The mediator should be asked whether or not he or she is willing to help in the court approval process (such as submitting an affidavit attesting to the fairness and thoroughness of the process involved in achieving agreement on a settlement).
- Damages often are difficult to assess; experts may need to play a role early on.
- Settlement will involve the negotiation of attorneys' fees. The parties should think carefully about when and how to negotiate this topic. Defendants need to be able to estimate the total cost of settlement; but given the need for court approval, the parties must avoid the appearance of impropriety.
  - How will attorneys' fees be estimated?
  - Address issues such as contingency, lodestar, multipliers, percentages, and clear sailing.
  - Applicable state or federal law will need to be carefully assessed because of variations in the requirements.
- Any settlement must address class notice, administration, and distribution issues.
  - Is there a common fund, claims-made or hybrid?
  - What happens when there is settlement money left over as a result of inability to locate class members, class member failure to file in time, or other issues?
    - Reversion (back to the defendants)?
    - Cy pres (such as distribution to a nonprofit consistent with the purpose of the class action)?
    - Redistributions to class members?

---

22. *See* FED. R. CIV. P. § 23(e)(2), *Approval of the Proposal.*

- Any settlement should address what happens if and when exposure to class members opting out of an approved settlement reaches an unacceptable level for defendants, e.g., "blow provisions" giving defendants the right to terminate or renegotiate upon meeting a threshold level of opt-out exposure (based upon the number of class members, potential dollar value of claims, or other measures).

9.8 What If Insurance Plays a Major Role in Settlement?

The role of an insurer in a mediation presents a number of special considerations. In effect, the mediation becomes a multiple-party one, and the insurer's perspective must be factored into the negotiation equation. J. Anderson Little's authoritative book *Making Money Talk: How to Mediate Insured Claims and Other Monetary Disputes* goes into much detail about the basics of bargaining over money, and we recommend it to anyone who faces this type of dispute on an ongoing basis.[23] We note the following points from our own experience:

- Depending on the circumstances, insurance companies often are in control of the litigation and settlement amounts. They are the "money" and will perform their own evaluation of the facts and the law.
- Claims representatives/adjusters are very experienced at mediation. They participate in hundreds of mediations a year.
- Although insurance companies have been at the forefront of using case analytics and automated negotiation ODR platforms such as Cybersettle, insurers were at first reluctant to participate by video in virtual Zoom mediations. This concern has eased significantly over time.
- Insurance representatives need—early on—information in connection with coverage, liability, and damages in order to get approval and authority to settle at amounts within policy limits. Policyholders need information about all the policies that may cover the loss at issue. All of this analysis requires lead time. Once again, preparation before the live session is critical, on both available policy, coverage, and damages issues. Exchanged mediation briefs, sent well before the live sessions, are an important way to communicate with all the stakeholders at the relevant insurance companies involved in analyzing the claim and authorizing settlement amounts. This is especially true in a pre-litigation situation.

23. Little, *supra* note 7.

Ultimately, insurers need to be involved in the design of the mediation process so that they are comfortable.

- The focus for the insurer is on whether the loss is covered under the policy, and then the value of the claim/case as affected by the costs of defense. These often are resolved as pure dollars disputes.
- Where insurance plays an important role in settlement, it is important for the advocates and ideal for the mediator to have a general understanding of key insurance principles such as the extent under state law or contract of an insurer's duty to defend (and the distinction between this and ultimate coverage issues), obligation to conduct a reasonable investigation, accept reasonable settlement amounts under policy limits, exposure to "bad faith" claims, the relationship between and among primary and excess insurers, and other issues that are seemingly collateral to the issues of liability and damages per se.
- Where insurance will figure largely in settlement, depending on the circumstances (including the continuation of court delays and closures due to the pandemic), it may be difficult to convince the insurer to conduct a very early mediation before some amount of litigation activity, including discovery and, if appropriate, expert reports. The insurer may believe it is unable to evaluate its exposure without a clear understanding of its risks at trial. As discussed, however, the mediation process can be used to some extent to substitute for discovery and help develop the parties' positions. In sophisticated mediations, expert reports can be prepared solely for mediation purposes.

9.9 Intellectual Property Disputes

Patent, trademark, trade secret, and copyright disputes among business partners or competitors are ideal candidates for mediation under most circumstances. These issues often are part of larger disputes in a business relationship.

Particularly in patent cases, but as is true in many intellectual property (IP) areas:

- The legal and technical questions that arise are complex, require extensive reliance on experts in court, and are therefore difficult and costly to litigate.
- Given these complexities, mediation can be helpful in preparing for and/or narrowing the issues that need to be litigated or arbitrated.

- Certainty with respect to one's IP rights is critical. Litigation outcomes are always uncertain, for a long period of time. A mediated solution provides certainty quickly and efficiently.
- The availability of remedies in mediation beyond winning or losing (injunctive relief or damages) can be very important. For example, the resolution of an IP dispute, whether directly negotiated or in mediation, often involves a business agreement and clarification of or modification to existing licenses or the negotiation of new or cross-licenses.
- A neutral mediator with expertise in transactions, technology, and/or a particular industry can be very advantageous in helping the parties see past their disagreements.
- The global scope of many IP disputes makes a non-litigation forum very helpful. If litigated, global patent disputes, for example, would require worldwide litigation.
- Confidentiality often is very important to the parties. For example, the mediation of a trade secret dispute permits the holder of the trade secret to reduce the risk—regardless of court-ordered sealing requirements—that the secret will be compromised. In a patent dispute, the ability to resolve a matter without a final and public finding regarding the validity of the patent may be a considerable benefit to the patent holder.

Preparation for IP mediation is even more important than usual given the complexities of the subject matter. In patent disputes, for example, the District Court of Massachusetts local rule for patent disputes sets forth a robust, excellent information exchange process that is in part designed to encourage early mediation. The rule requires that both parties exchange extensive information about the patent claims and infringement and defenses early in the case.[24] Suffice it to say that understanding and refuting invalidity defenses such as obviousness can take quite some time and can and should be conducted over several sessions. The mediator can be used to protect confidential outside counsel opinions.

In addition, the parties in complex technical cases should consider whether or not retaining a joint, neutral expert to prepare reports or opinions solely for mediation is appropriate and will help resolve the dispute before litigation or arbitration is commenced.

24. See https://www.mad.uscourts.gov › pdf › local-rules.

There are several situations in which mediation is unlikely to be an effective process. First, the holder of IP rights may need to set a precedent and establish the metes and bounds of their "property right" against all comers; in this case, litigation is the only option. Second, so-called patent trolls or other holders of IP rights who are not interested in a business solution, but rather, are simply looking to monetize their rights, may not be interested in a settlement that makes business sense to the party accused of infringing the right. Last but not least, a competitor may see a significant interest in a scorched-earth litigation strategy against their adversary.

Of note, the Internet Corporation for Assigned Names and Numbers, the entity that among other things governs the registration of domain names for internet sites, long ago set up a required arbitration process for the resolution of trademark owner claims of abusive registration filings (such as cybersquatting). Approved arbitration providers for this program include the World Intellectual Property Organization.

Chapter 10
Case Studies in Commercial Mediation

10.1 Introduction

The following case studies offer concrete examples of why mediation is becoming more attractive as a dispute resolution alternative.

10.2 Major Bank vs. High-Tech Computer Corporation

A high-tech company entered into a contract with a major bank to provide a new software program designed to revolutionize accounting systems within the bank's trust department and to make the department far more profitable. After the high-tech company failed several times to meet projected delivery schedules, the bank filed a lawsuit for breach of contract, seeking recovery of all monies paid and other consequential damages.

Before proceeding with lengthy and costly discovery, the parties agreed to devote one day to mediation. The mediator began by asking both parties to argue the merits of their respective positions. The presidents of both companies and their counsel attended the joint session. In the first caucus session with the bank, the mediator learned that the bank had not lost confidence in the software company's ultimate ability to provide the product consistent with the bank's needs and specifications. However, the bank had serious concerns about the software company's ability to meet its deadlines.

In the first caucus session with the software company, the mediator learned that the company needed time to work out problems within the system, that it was confident about its ability to perform in a timely manner, and that other banks were lined up to purchase the system if it worked as advertised. The mediator learned further that the potentially lucrative future of the company depended on the successful completion of this first installation.

Over a two-day period (notwithstanding the initial agreement to mediate for only a day), the mediator was able to work directly with the parties to restructure their relationship. The software company was given additional time to complete the contract. Additionally, the terms between the parties were changed to give the bank (1) a slightly lower price for the software, and (2) an interest in the software company's profits from future installations over a period of years.

10.3 Insolvent Bank vs. Law Firm

A receiver was appointed by the court to govern the liquidation of an insolvent bank. Shortly after his appointment, the receiver reviewed the affairs of the bank for the decade preceding his appointment. He concluded that the insolvency would not have occurred but for the conduct of the law firm that had served as principal counsel to the bank.

The receiver filed a malpractice suit in the U.S. District Court, laying the blame for the demise of the bank at the doorstep of the law firm. More specifically, the complaint alleged that a partner of the law firm who served on the bank's board of directors failed to uncover mismanagement and self-dealing on the part of the bank's principal officers. Adopting a "hear no evil, see no evil" approach to service on the board, the partner's inaction allegedly permitted management to remain entrenched and thus permitted what the complaint called the "looting" to continue. Throughout the decade, the law firm earned millions of dollars in fees for its legal services to the bank. The complaint alleged that the law firm's conduct constituted a conflict of interest, breach of contract, fraud, and breach of fiduciary duties.

After four years of multiple motions and scores of depositions, the presiding judge ordered the parties to participate in private mediation. At the inception of the mediation, the plaintiff demanded "tens of millions" of dollars. Because the defendants regarded the lawsuit as wholly without merit, this demand was met with the response of "not a penny."

After permitting the parties to argue the merits of their positions for a few hours, the mediator challenged both parties in private caucuses to make a more realistic assessment of their case. The mediator spent hours with the parties exploring the weaknesses of their respective cases and assessing the likely risks and costs at trial. After this process, the mediator challenged the plaintiff to lower its demand and defendants to make a credible offer. The mediator urged both parties to send the first signal, explaining the negotiating theory that suggests that the party making the first "credible" move can achieve a significant benefit.

Later that day, after almost eight hours of meeting in joint and caucus sessions, the defendants finally made an offer of more than "nuisance value." In response, plaintiff lowered its demand by a small amount. Defendants were persuaded to increase their offer, even though they did so by only a small amount. The mediator then maintained the momentum by persuading the parties to make a significant number of small moves. Late in the evening, as a result of this signaling process, the dispute was settled in what is called a "tit for tat" negotiation.

In sum, the "case which could not be settled" was resolved because the mediator (1) challenged both sides in caucus sessions to recognize their weaknesses and reassess their positions, (2) persevered, even when the parties viewed the situation as hopeless, and (3) offered the parties assistance with their negotiating strategies. Even in a difficult pure dollars dispute such as this one, the mediator was able to establish a level of communication that the parties had been unable to achieve on their own. As a consequence of the mediator's patience, determination, and continued optimism, the parties remained together for over twelve hours. In an unassisted negotiation, it is likely that one of the parties would have abandoned the process.

10.4 Accounting Firm vs. Departing Partners

An accounting firm was experiencing significant difficulties among its partners over important strategic issues. After some debate within the partnership, the partners decided to remain together and seek the professional services of a consulting firm to consider the continued viability of the firm. Within several weeks, several partners abruptly left to establish their own competing firm.

The breakup of the accounting practice resulted in numerous charges and countercharges from both groups over issues such as (1) entitlement to profits, (2) responsibility for debts, and (3) control of client accounts. In addition, the accounting firm charged the departing partners with breaching their fiduciary duties by allegedly "parking" opportunities and writing off time.

Both groups retained attorneys and threatened to sue for various claims. The parties, however, agreed to try mediation first. A mediator was able to overcome the emotional hostilities and get beyond the legal posturing by impressing upon all parties the need to resolve the dispute promptly, confidentially, and in the interests of the clients of all parties. The mediator was able to resolve not only the monetary issues, but also was able to seek agreement on many additional issues likely to arise, including some of the boundaries of future competition.

10.5 Shareholder Dispute Among Family Members

A substantial family business was owned by four brothers and sisters who had inherited their interests from their father. Each of the four owned 25 percent of the shares in the company.

For more than five years, the oldest brother had served as president and CEO of the company. During this period, although the value of the business continually declined, the president's salary and travel and entertainment budget increased. The siblings who were not actively involved in the business questioned whether their brother's level of income was warranted given the company's financial picture. However, they were unwilling to make any formal challenge because of their concern that their brother, the only one who knew how to run the business, would quit.

When the business continued to deteriorate, one of the brothers challenged his oldest brother and threatened legal action. Because of this challenge, the two brothers stopped talking to each other. An accountant who had served the company for two generations suggested voluntary mediation. All parties agreed.

A mediator was able to recognize that long-standing jealousies and other family issues played as large a role in the dispute as the business and legal issues. After allowing all the parties to express their feelings and state their positions, the mediator suggested a number of proposals. In the latter part of the session, an apology from the oldest brother for being too "high-handed" in his management style went a long way toward bringing the parties together. Ultimately, all four agreed to resolve their dispute by selling the business and dividing the net proceeds.

10.6 Defense Contractor vs. Supplier

Two large, multinational corporations, embroiled in costly litigation for over two years, turned to mediation as an alternative. The litigation was commenced when a defense contractor sued a supplier for breach of contract, alleging the supplier's failure to meet its deadlines under the contract. As a consequence, the contractor was forced to obtain the necessary component parts from a second source at a much higher price. The complaint sought damages for the difference in price.

The supplier contended that errors in the contractor's performance specifications made performance within the contract's stated deadlines an impossibility. The supplier filed a counterclaim for its payments due under the contract.

Approximately six months prior to trial, the presiding judge scheduled a pretrial conference to resolve the outstanding pretrial issues and to explore settlement. Counsel for both parties were instructed to discuss settlement with their respective clients prior to the court conference. Upon being approached by outside counsel, general counsel for the plaintiff expressed her concern over mounting legal fees and expenses. She further expressed the concern of the company's chief executive officer that the dispute was preventing discussion of other joint ventures with the supplier elsewhere in the world. Outside counsel for the contractor was instructed by the general counsel to suggest voluntary mediation to counsel for the supplier.

The general counsel noted that both corporations had signed the ADR pledge of the CPR Institute, requiring the consideration of alternatives to litigation, where appropriate. She specifically suggested to outside counsel that this pledge, signed before the dispute arose, be mentioned to opposing counsel.

The supplier agreed to participate in the suggested mediation. In the initial joint session, both parties argued the merits of their respective legal positions. However, in private caucus sessions, both parties quickly conceded their desire to compromise the dispute. This concession was driven on both sides by (1) increasing fees and costs, and (2) the recognition that the parties were unlikely to be able to pursue future joint ventures if the litigation continued and the level of trust between the parties continued to deteriorate.

Although outside counsel and high-level inside corporate counsel attended the mediation, the mediator was unable to resolve the dispute at the mediation session. He was unable to give the parties the one ingredient they both needed—time. Both sides needed more time to reevaluate their settlement positions. However, several weeks later, the parties decided that the chief executives of both companies should meet to continue the settlement negotiations. The dispute was resolved at this meeting, primarily because of the foundation provided by the voluntary mediation.

10.7 Pharmaceutical Product Seller vs. Pharmaceutical Product Buyer—Manufacturing Issues

A large pharmaceutical company sold a portfolio of products to a startup. The products were sold in a number of European countries. The large pharmaceutical company also agreed to a transitional manufacturing agreement to permit the startup company to secure third-party manufacturing capability. One of the higher-value products in the portfolio developed a "stability" issue, meaning that the product might not meet regulatory requirements for sale. The parties attempted to resolve the problem, but ultimately the product was withdrawn from the market.

The parties traded business and then legal communications regarding responsibility for the problem under the sale agreement and the transitional manufacturing agreement, and then decided to retain a mediator experienced in the industry to help them resolve the issues before the buyer filed for arbitration.

The mediation proceeded virtually on the Zoom platform. Extensive position and information exchange was encouraged by the mediator prior to the initial Zoom session. That initial session involved participants from eight countries, including legal, manufacturing, marketing, business development, and other executives. At the suggestion of the mediator, the parties explored, in addition to liability risk, both cash value exchanges related to future profits lost and the possible transfer of additional products or discounts on products outside of those transferred in order to resolve the issues. Additional information exchanges followed. Additional Zoom sessions involving only inside counsel and business executives, using the information secured during the mediation process, and the mediator's and outside counsel's evaluation of each side's risks, resulted in a settlement satisfactory to both sides.

10.8 Medical Device Company Seller vs. Medical Device Company Buyer—Earn-Outs

A small, family-owned device company selling products to hospitals sold its entire business to a large, European-based device company. The principals of the small company agreed to perform consulting services to help the larger company sell the devices in the complex and highly regulated hospital market. The sale agreement provided that upon the achievement of sales targets, the principals would receive substantial earn-outs above the agreed initial purchase price. A two-page operating plan set forth expectations for the buyer's efforts. The targets were not met, and the sellers accused the buyers of failing to put sufficient effort into meeting the sales targets. The buyers accused the sellers of interfering with the management of the buyers' sales efforts.

The parties agreed to mediate before any litigation had been filed. The mediator convinced the parties to engage in extensive information exchange and used her familiarity with the industry to help set expectations for performance of the buyer, the documentation of the parties' obligations, and the reasonable differences in priorities between a small company focused on the small number of products sold by the small company and—without clear contractual expectations to the contrary—the larger company. The sophisticated principals agreed to walk from the controversy without any additional financial compensation given the misunderstandings, differences in perspectives, and expense of litigation, and the principals thanked the mediator for her candor.

10.9 Healthcare Insurer vs. Healthcare Provider

A hospital system complained that a health insurer had inappropriately denied emergency room payments at a certain level of care, and therefore had provided insufficient reimbursement to the provider. The parties had resolved these issues on a going-forward basis, and the issue was how to resolve the dispute with respect to hundreds of past claims for in-network emergency services based upon the contractual provisions governing reimbursement and the industry-standard coding and definitions applicable to the services. The parties engaged in extensive preparation, exchanging information and key documents with the mediator, and prepared for a virtual Zoom arbitration. Participants by Zoom included inside and outside counsel and businesspeople. The mediator assisted each side in assessing risk in an ensuing arbitration, and the parties reached an amicable resolution with respect to the past claims in a 12-hour virtual session.

10.10 Pharmacy Benefit Management Company vs. Pharmaceutical Company

A pharmaceutical company performed an audit of a pharmacy benefit management company and believed that it had found evidence of inappropriate rebate payments that were not qualified for reimbursement under the companies' numerous agreements over the years. The parties engaged exchanged audit documents, background information about the development of the contractual relationship, and participated in a Zoom mediation involving inside and outside counsel, auditors, and business executives. Multiple smaller sessions among experts helped narrow and identify the issues, and the parties reached an amicable resolution one week after the initial Zoom session.

10.11 Multi-Party Dispute Involving Inventors, University, and Startup Company

Two scientists, one employed by a university and another employed by a pharmaceutical startup, had worked together on related technology at the university scientist's lab. The startup scientist had continued and modified that work, and he filed patents relating to the technology, ultimately licensing his work to the pharmaceutical startup. The pharmaceutical startup was developing and hoped to commercialize a product based upon the patented technology. A dispute arose as to whether or not the university scientist was entitled to be named as an inventor on the underlying patents and possibly participate in the earnings of the pharmaceutical company of any products were approved.

Over many preparation sessions discussing the original work done by the scientists, the technology as it was developed, the scope of the issued patents, patent applications and continuations, live sessions, and follow-up negotiations of three separate agreements, with the help of the mediator, the parties resolved their complex dispute.

CHAPTER 11
CORPORATE AND LAW FIRM ADR STRATEGIES

11.1 Introduction

Many corporations have reacted to the significant risks and costs of resolving disputes and have begun implementing conflict management strategies and programs designed to resolve conflicts at the earliest stage possible. (A law firm-wide ADR culture remains the exception. The law firm that assumes a leadership role on these issues, however, will have a significant advantage in the legal marketplace as we begin the 21st century.)

11.2 Corporate Dispute Prevention and Resolution Strategies

The elements of a corporate dispute prevention and resolution program can vary significantly, depending on the objectives and culture of a particular corporation. There are certain elements and practices that are likely to enhance the success of any such program. The following "best practices" in dispute resolution are offered as a guide to corporations desiring to make such a commitment.[25]

11.2.1 Perform a Dispute Audit

In order to understand the needs of your organization, one overlooked device is to perform an audit of the number, type, and duration of disputes with business partners that required significant senior management attention and how these disputes were resolved. How might these disputes have been avoided, and would it have been helpful to have a multi-step clause requiring negotiation, mediation, and arbitration in any underlying agreement? Obviously, this type of data gathering will need to be highly customized, but

25. Section 9.2 on best practices in corporate ADR is adapted from Jack L. Foltz & Bennett G. Picker, *Alternative Dispute Resolution*, *in* SUCCESSFUL PARTNERING BETWEEN INSIDE AND OUTSIDE COUNSEL §57:1-57:74 (Robert L. Haig ed., 2000).

a lessons-learned approach to building a dispute prevention and resolution program will result in a program that meets the particularized needs of the company.

11.2.2 Secure the Buy-In of Management

For a corporate dispute prevention and resolution program to be successful, key executives in a company need to understand the economic benefits of resolving disputes without significant arbitration or litigation. The dispute audit recommended above can be helpful in appreciating those benefits and the cost to the company of addressing business partner disputes. Absent such an understanding, many executives initially take a win-at-any-cost approach until they begin to appreciate the substantial risks and costs of litigation. Executives should be made aware of the particular advantages of dispute prevention and resolution, including the potential for early disposition of disputes, the substantial savings in litigation costs, the desirability of avoiding the distractions of litigation, the benefits of privacy and confidentiality and, perhaps most importantly, the potential for business solutions that will serve the bottom-line interests of the company.

11.2.3 Commit Resources for Dispute Prevention and Resolution Education and Training

An upfront investment of time and money is necessary for a dispute prevention and resolution program to succeed. In order for the law department and key executives to understand the benefits, training programs should be offered to enable these persons to understand the full range of options available to avoid, manage, and resolve disputes. Companies should also make available books, periodicals, treatises, model policies, and forms in order for key personnel to understand the important issues in the field and take a sophisticated approach in commercial transactions. Organizations such as the CPR Institute, the AAA, JAMS, and the ABA can either provide or recommend highly qualified persons to conduct training programs.

11.2.4 Establish an In-House Advocate for Dispute Prevention and Resolution

The company should designate one person as the in-house advocate for prevention and resolution processes. Although this person may have other responsibilities, he or she can be responsible for establishing systems to avoid disputes, establishing policies for a sophisticated approach to commercial agreements, incorporating appropriate mechanisms into the company's policies for retention of outside counsel, and designing programs for early case assessment. The advocate should try to motivate people across departmental lines and encourage the establishment of pertinent policies and practices that will serve the best interests of the company.

11.2.5 Focus on Dispute Prevention

As previously noted, participants in complex industries such as construction and the life sciences have long looked to prevent disputes from arising in the first place through methods such as partnering, alliance and relationship management, committee structures, dispute resolution boards, and other mechanisms that permit the real-time avoidance of disputes. Focusing on a systematic dispute prevention approach is wise.

In 2021, the CPR Institute rolled out a new pledge, *Dispute Prevention for Business Partners*:

> To preserve relationships in business arrangements, and subject to mutually agreed-upon terms, we will incorporate dispute prevention mechanisms into our arrangements where appropriate. The range of mechanisms may include, for example, reliance upon resources internal to the parties, such as prompt escalation of conflicts within and between organizations, or third-party mechanisms, such as jointly engaging a dispute prevention neutral; all designed to enable early identification of conflict and preventing it from hardening into a dispute. This statement of policy does not commit us to any particular outcome, but only to the willingness jointly to deploy dispute prevention mechanisms to help us avoid disputes and maintain our business relationships and purpose.[26]

The CPR Institute Dispute Prevention Task Force is in the process of developing training and other materials to assist companies in implementing this pledge.

11.2.6 Sign the CPR Institute Corporate Policy Statement on Alternatives to Litigation

The CPR Institute Corporate Policy on Alternatives to Litigation can serve as a signal to business partners of your organization's intentions to use

26. See https://www.cpradr.org/resource-center/adr-pledges.

mediation and arbitration and other dispute resolution tools to resolve disputes:

> We recognize that for many disputes there is a less expensive, more effective method of resolution than the traditional lawsuit. Alternative dispute resolution (ADR) procedures involve collaborative techniques which often can spare businesses the high costs of litigation.
>
> In recognition of the foregoing, we subscribe to the following statements of principle on behalf of our company and its domestic subsidiaries:
>
> In the event of a business dispute between our company and another company which has made or will then make a similar statement, we are prepared to explore with that other party resolution of the dispute through negotiation or ADR techniques before pursuing full-scale litigation. If either party believes that the dispute is not suitable for ADR techniques, or if such techniques do not produce results satisfactory to the disputants, either party may proceed with litigation.[27]

Or, your company can sign the CPR Institute 21st Century Pledge:

> Our company pledges to commit its resources to manage and resolve disputes through negotiation, mediation and other ADR processes when appropriate, with a view to establishing and practicing global, sustainable dispute management and resolution processes.[28]

11.2.7 Insist That Outside Counsel Address Dispute Prevention and Resolution

Companies should consider respectfully insisting that their outside law firms sign the CPR Institute Law Firm Policy Statement Alternatives to Litigation, which states:

> We recognize that for many disputes there may be methods more effective for resolution than traditional litigation. Alternative dispute resolution procedures—used in conjunction with litigation or independently—can significantly reduce the cost and burdens of litigation and result in solutions not available in court. In recognition of the foregoing, we

27. See https://www.cpradr.org/resource-center/adr-pledges/corporate-policy-statement.
28. See https://www.cpradr.org/resource-center/adr-pledges/21st-century-pledge.

> subscribe to the following statements of policy on behalf of our firm. First, appropriate lawyers in our firm will be knowledgeable about ADR. Second, where appropriate, the responsible attorney will discuss with the client the availability of ADR procedures so the client can make an informed choice concerning resolution of the dispute.[29]

In addition, companies should ask their outside law firms what measures they have undertaken to make this pledge a reality. More specifically, they should ask what formal training has been provided to the firm and whether there is an ADR practice group or individuals within the firm to serve as advisors at more sophisticated levels, both to the client and to other firm members.

At a very minimum, a company should insist in its retention letter that outside counsel recommend dispute resolution options, where appropriate. Additionally, many companies have adopted early case evaluation protocols that require their outside law firms, at an early stage of every dispute, to provide a written assessment of the risks and costs of litigation and any recommended ADR strategies. Some companies, before permitting a case to continue in litigation, have adopted formal policies requiring their outside law firms, within 90 days of making a claim or filing litigation, to make an assessment of why a case is inappropriate for ADR.

Finally, and in keeping with an emphasis on dispute prevention, inside counsel should focus their efforts on transactional lawyers who are drafting their business arrangements with third parties and discuss how to implement techniques that will prevent disputes from arising in the first place. These could include the appointment of relationship or alliance managers, the establishment of committees specifically charged with improving communications, and the use of standing neutrals, as previously noted.

11.2.8 Establish a Suitability Screen to Determine Whether the Case Is Appropriate for Mediation, Arbitration, and Other Dispute Prevention and Resolution Techniques

Companies should develop a "suitability screen" to assist in determining whether a case is appropriate for mediation or some other non-traditional dispute prevention or resolution alternative. Suitability screens have been

---

29. See https://www.cpradr.org/resource-center/adr-pledges/law-firm-policy-statement.

adopted by the CPR Institute and a number of companies and law firms. These screens provide checklists to permit lawyers to determine whether a business dispute is suitable for resolution through ADR. The screens ask questions relating to the parties to the dispute, the role of counsel, the interests the parties are advancing, and the outcomes the parties are seeking. Examples of such questions include the following:

- Are parties members of the CPR Institute or other industry-based ADR pact?
- Would a presentation by one party's counsel to the other side promote a more realistic case assessment?
- Is confidentiality important?
- Do the parties seek a resolution that a court could not order?

11.2.9 Incorporate Dispute Prevention and Multi-Tiered Dispute Resolution Provisions in Contracts

Many companies historically have inserted a boilerplate arbitration clause in commercial agreements to provide an alternative to litigation. Companies should take a far more sophisticated approach and, depending on the transaction, consider self-help mechanisms such as the appointment of relationship or alliance managers, joint project committees, and a multi-tiered approach calling for neutral fact-finding, executive negotiations, and mediation as a predicate to either arbitration or litigation. Dispute resolution clauses in commercial agreements are not one-size-fits-all. The kind of dispute likely to arise should dictate the preferred dispute resolution option in a commercial agreement, as illustrated by the following examples:

- Will the client want a quick, negotiated resolution? (Mediation)
- Is there a non-negotiable interest that needs protection? (Litigation)
- Will there likely be a large volume of small-dollar disputes? (Arbitration)
- Will there be a small number of big-dollar disputes? (Mediation)
- Is the transaction a cross-border one? (Arbitration)

Dispute resolution clauses should be inserted in early drafts of agreements where they can be given the full attention they deserve. In drafting dispute resolution clauses, a company should create a checklist that reflects its particular business concerns and focuses on the key legal issues. This list can be informed by the dispute audit that we recommend above. We will note that, in our view, there is no downside to having a well-drafted mediation clause in all contractual arrangements of any significance.

11.2.10 Use Negotiation and Mediation As Tools to Resolve Disputes

In focusing on dispute prevention and resolution, in addition to building in mechanisms to prevent disputes from arising in the first place, companies should not overlook the possibility of direct and unassisted negotiations as the initial path to resolution of a dispute. Any dispute appropriate for a negotiated resolution is also appropriate for mediation. Mediation should be considered, wherever possible, as a powerful tool to resolve disputes early, cost-effectively, and fairly. Mediators can focus on the underlying business interests of the parties and attempt to fashion solutions that advance both sets of interests, rather than merely vindicating the rights of one party. In many situations, a skilled mediator can overcome the barriers that have arisen in an unassisted negotiation and facilitate creative, business-driven solutions that are simply unavailable in the win-lose environment of litigation.

11.2.11 Encourage Adversaries to Use Dispute Prevention and Resolution Techniques

Any company that has made a major internal commitment to adopt a dispute prevention and resolution approach should have, as one of its goals, motivating its adversaries to use similar mechanisms. Some companies are reluctant to suggest ADR or mediation to an adversary for fear of showing weakness and losing leverage in negotiations. Properly presented, however, this should not be a major concern. At the appropriate juncture in a dispute, a company can suggest mediation by stating, "We're so sure a mediator will validate the strength of our position that we're willing to take the risk we are wrong." If the adversary is reluctant because of its unfamiliarity with ADR or mediation, neutral organizations such as the CPR Institute have a good track record of convincing parties of the benefits of ADR. Where adversaries have signed the CPR Institute pledge to use ADR or a similar pledge in an industry treaty, parties can be reminded of these commitments made prior to the existence of a dispute. Since mediation is nonbinding, parties can consider giving the adversary a fair degree of control over decisions such as the designation of the neutral or the recommendation of procedures.

11.2.12 Litigate When Necessary

When there is the need to defend a frivolous case, to file an injunction, to establish a precedent, or to protect a strategic interest, litigation may well be the best option. Discovery and motion practice remain important tools in litigation. There is simply no substitute for good case preparation and strong trial skills. Moreover, a readiness to litigate when appropriate will permit a party to negotiate in an ADR setting from a position of strength. The initial decision to litigate, however, should be reviewed at every critical stage of the litigation process. Even after litigation has commenced, mediation may still offer the most direct and least costly path toward a favorable result.

11.2.13 Be Patient; Track and Measure the Results

Once a company places well-drawn ADR provisions in its commercial agreements and employment manual, some time may elapse before a dispute arises that is covered by the new language. Therefore, it may be some time before a company can determine whether it is in a position to achieve earlier and less expensive resolutions in a private manner. Some companies have reported publicly that the widespread use of ADR techniques has resulted in the reduction of claims and proceedings (measured in the thousands) and savings of defense expenses and settlement payments (measured in the millions) each year. Take the time to measure and record the results and to compare them to the cost and time associated with disputes resolved in litigation. It takes time to build a successful program, and not every dispute resolution experience will be positive. Over time, however, focusing on prevention and dispute resolution should yield substantial benefits.

11.3 Law Firm ADR Strategies

More than 1,500 law firms have signed the CPR Institute Law Firm Policy Statement on Alternatives to Litigation. This commitment requires firm lawyers to be knowledgeable about ADR and, where appropriate, discuss with the client the advisability of ADR procedures, so the client can make a reasoned choice concerning the resolution of the dispute.

In order to breathe life into this pledge, however, a law firm needs to make a meaningful commitment to provide dispute prevention and resolution counseling and advocacy services at sophisticated levels. The CPR Institute has developed a multi-step program for law firms seeking to systematically include ADR in the dispute management services offered to clients.[30] The following is an outline of this program:

- *ADR structures and policies*
  - Organize an ADR planning committee and ADR department. We have seen a number of law firms set up "dispute resolution" committee.
  - Appoint a senior partner as ADR counsel.
  - Adopt a law firm ADR policy statement.
- *Tailored ADR training and resources*
  - Address common ADR obstacles.
  - Enlist support of the firm's ADR practitioners.
  - Provide ADR training and resources.
  - Encourage ADR research.
- *Systematic ADR case analysis*
  - Develop suitability screens.
  - Promote use of ADR in contract clauses.
- *Full range of ADR services*
  - Educate clients and market the firm's ADR services.
  - Establish ADR billing policies.
  - Offer ADR advocacy, counseling, and neutral services.
- *ADR advocacy strategies*
  - Probe client's interest in ADR.
  - Get parties to the negotiating table.
  - Tailor ADR processes to case needs.
  - Limit ADR discovery practice.
  - Select client representatives for ADR.
  - Prepare for mediation and arbitration sessions.
- *ADR tracking practices*
  - Develop closed-case routines.
  - Create tracking forms and catalogue the data

These strategies are intended for larger firms that want to promote a firm-wide culture that embraces an ADR approach to conflict management and dispute resolution. At the very least, every law firm should have an appreciation for the landscape of ADR—including the increased emphasis on dispute prevention, as well as resolution—and the advantages offered

30. *See* CRONIN-HARRIS, CATHERINE, *BUILDING ADR INTO THE LAW FIRM* (1997).

by mediating business disputes. Even in smaller firms, one or more lawyers can assume the responsibility for understanding the suitability, preparation, and advocacy issues at sophisticated levels. Whatever the size of the firm, every lawyer engaged in resolving business disputes can achieve significant benefits for the client by systematically including mediation as a dispute resolution alternative in the appropriate case.

Chapter 12
Reflections on How We Got Here

12.1 Introduction

The co-authors of this book took very different paths to get to similar points as mediators (and arbitrators). As we worked through the revisions for this edition, we have been amazed at the similarities in our approaches. We thought that readers, especially those considering mediation as a career, might be interested in our paths and our reflections on our work. These thoughts are very personal but, we hope, helpful to those thinking about the field as either an advocate or a neutral.

12.2 Bennett G. Picker

When I was a young lawyer in the early 1970s and I was about to try my first case, I represented a defendant in connection with a claim arising from an alleged breach of a long-term supply agreement. Six weeks before trial, the parties and counsel agreed to a one-time meeting to explore settlement. At this meeting, Plaintiff's counsel made an excessively high demand. My client said, "They're not here in good faith. Let's walk out."

In response to my urging that we make a credible offer, my client responded, "I thought you were my lawyer. If you don't believe in my case, maybe I should find another lawyer." Needless to say, our effort to settle was an abysmal failure. I walked away from our meeting thinking, *if only*. If only an intermediary were present to work with both parties, perhaps we might have settled by restructuring the agreement on different pricing terms. Although my client prevailed, in part, at trial, he was displeased with both the result and the cost.

So, why did we not consider mediation? The answer is that the process never crossed our minds. In the early 1970s, mediation of commercial cases simply did not exist. Then, in a five-year period, the landscape of mediation changed dramatically. In what I have described as a "perfect rainbow," the process was advanced by the Pound Conference, convened in 1976 by Chief Justice Warren Burger, at which the Harvard law professor articulated the concept of a multi-door courthouse that included mediation. In 1977, the CPR Institute was formed by corporate counsel looking for faster, better, and cheaper ways to resolve disputes. I believe that the CPR Institute was largely responsible for institutionalizing mediation in corporate and law firm settings during the 1980s and 1990s, and it continues to be a center for developing best practices in mediation. In 1981, the process of mediation was popularized by Roger Fisher and William Ury's book *Getting to Yes*,[31] which identified mediation's potential for interest-based and even win-win solutions to business disputes.

My own world changed in the 1980s as I quickly saw the potential for creative solutions to business disputes—solutions not available in either litigation or arbitration. I began thinking about changing my own practice and wanted to learn more about mediation. I was then fortunate to take a course taught by two of the great masters of mediation, Michael Lewis and Linda Singer, a course my co-author Conna also took and greatly admired. As Chancellor of the Philadelphia Bar Association in the mid-1980s, I was regularly called upon to help facilitate the resolution of both private and public disputes. It did not take me too long to realize that while opposing lawyers would argue their best positions in every dispute, the disputes were invariably as much about the people and the problem as they were about the positions. So, in the late 1980s, I decided to develop a strategic plan to transition my practice to full-time work as a mediator.

31. *See* FISHER, *supra* note 9.

When I started to mediate in the 1980s, I was just one of three or four lawyers holding themselves out as mediators. Today, while it is difficult to count, I believe there are more than 500 such individuals in my region. I consider myself blessed to be a full-time mediator. I am called upon to apply the skills of a litigator, a negotiator, an advocate, a counsellor, a diplomat, and a psychologist. Serving as a mediator has its own set of challenges, such as the need to recall after the sixth or seventh hour precisely what information is or is not confidential; the need to explore the underlying barriers and drivers of resolutions; the need to explore the depths or personal and business relationships; the need to identify; and the need for endless amounts of perseverance and optimism necessary to bring parties together. I have also come to recognize the critical importance of preparation, of fairness, and of respect for the process.

In a word, I feel "lucky" to participate in a process where I get paid to help people solve their problems in ways that at times appear to be almost magical. For that reason, I never lost my passion for the process—and I know my co-author Conna shares this passion for the craft. At the same time, I lament that we seem to have less focus on the words that defined the process in the early years, such as "collaboration" and "creativity." I regret that the "safe place" for conversation we all cherished several decades ago has become a forum that is, at times, more about bargaining for advantage. At the same time, I see how much we have gained over the past few decades with widespread education and almost universal acceptance of the process, greater opportunities for professional collegiality, and greater diversity.

I have seen the process change in so many ways over the years. Who would have predicted that an intensely personal process could be successful on a virtual basis (in fact, there was not even an internet when I started serving as a mediator). So, I am reluctant to make predictions about how the process will change in the future. What we do know is that the process will continue to change and in ways that we cannot anticipate. But change we must or, to paraphrase Professor Sander, "our profession will be killed by the status quo."

At the end of the day, when I try to predict where we will be in five years, I am optimistic. After all, I am a mediator, and optimism is what we are all about.

12.3 Conna A. Weiner

When I was a litigator at a New York law firm in the late 1980s and early 1990s, I lived in a world of lawyers and by the choreography of litigation. I received fantastic training from some of the best minds in the litigation business. I focused on procedure, an intense analysis of the past, deciding who was right and wrong—and more or less demonizing the "other side." I noticed that some of the matters I started with remained on my desk for quite some time, including an international arbitration that took three years and had full-scale discovery since the lawyers running the case decided to adopt the Federal Rules of Civil Procedure. I also noticed the exacerbation of conflict as litigators stepped in and prepared for battle. I wondered if there was a better way to resolve business disputes, especially those that were not bet-the-company cases and involved ongoing relationships. (And I wondered what kind of person I was becoming as my poor non-lawyer friends accused me of deposing them over dinner.)

So, I backed away from a steady diet of disputes to broaden my world and learn to become a business lawyer helping clients look to the future, build things, achieve their business objectives, and solve problems—and, with any luck, avoiding the creation of new disputes (and new business) for my old litigator colleagues. For me, this meant going in-house to the life sciences and healthcare industries.

The transition from being a law firm litigator to being an in-house corporate lawyer in a complex industry was mind-bogglingly scary on a bad day and transformative on a good one. Readers who have made the same jump will know what it is like—going from being at the top of the food chain in a law firm to a perceived "cost center" blocking progress and holding things up; the need to make quick, highly triaged judgments and risk-assessments based upon very little information, not to mention very little legal research; appreciating the importance of knowing your industry inside and out, including the esoteric world of patents and other innovation industry subjects; learning (with the help of wonderful outside counsel experts) to draft complex contracts governing years-long research; development and commercialization collaborations; global supply deals or mergers and acquisitions; fighting for resources; managing outside counsel; attempting to navigate internal politics without getting run over oneself; and in my case, living and working outside the United States . . . it was really quite something. I even had to learn to play a little golf (thank you to the wonderful Eric Snedecor, formerly of Novartis and now retired).

One lesson I learned early on was just how unimportant I was, and how unimportant mere appearances were, compared to the tremendous competence of the business people and scientists who were actually attempting to bring life-saving pharmaceuticals, medical devices, and diagnostics to the market. On one of my first days on the job, I was asked to help investigate alleged contamination at one of the manufacturing sites of my employer, which might have to result in a product recall. Could we get away without the recall? What should we tell the regulators?

Someone walked into my office with a mullet haircut, chewing and popping purple gum, and sporting long, matching fingernails. Costumed in my finest, sharp New York City suit and heels, I began to ask her a few questions about the incident, and she proceeded to utterly overwhelm me with her attention to detail, command of the facts, technical expertise, and commitment to integrity. I never wore that suit again. I learned who was really in charge. It (and many experiences like these, including counterparties) is why I respectfully press for extensive business client involvement in all of my mediations.

After training as a mediator and an arbitrator, I realized that I had in fact been informally developing those skills, in fits and starts to be sure, throughout my inside counsel career. Working closely with so many different functions, persuading internal clients to involve their lawyers early and often, running cross-functional projects, and working with external partners on value-expanding deals—eventually I left behind my automatic characterization of lawyers from other companies as the other side and appreciated viscerally just how important it was to credit different perspectives. You can read that this is true in negotiation books, but you have to live it, over many years, to really get it. I have often told young lawyers that a law firm–inside counsel career path is terrific training for a next transition from being an advocate to being a business-focused neutral capable of seeing all sides and bringing a business solution perspective to bear on the dispute. At some point, you cross the threshold and look at things in a new way. And appreciating the strangle-hold that corporate politics can have over legal departments and business people can help mediators who have been there provide a navigational assist to disputing parties.

And with my co-author Ben, I truly feel that it is a gift and an honor actually to be able to serve as a mediator and an arbitrator for a living (although I try not to do a mediation and an arbitration "thing" on the same day, as they require very different approaches!) The emphasis for both of us is on the word *serve*. For each mediation, for example, all of my accumulated lenses—as a litigator, inside counsel, business counselor, and arbitrator, as well as a mediator—go into ensuring that my mediation clients, the business people and their lawyers, are taking their next step with fully informed consent. It takes everything I've got professionally, and it's a joy.

12.4 The Rewards of Adding Value

While there are many new challenges in the mediation field, there are also new opportunities and new rewards. The world of dispute resolution and prevention, unbounded by strict rules of litigation, is limited only by one's imagination. Lawyers and their clients are designing new and imaginative approaches to dispute resolution every day.

For both corporate counsel and the private bar, a problem-solving approach to dispute prevention and resolution can be extraordinarily stimulating and rewarding. Each next case requires a fresh new approach, an understanding of the client's business and objectives, and far more communication with the client. The COVID-19 pandemic has only heightened the need for new and flexible approaches to disputes. As we move forward, we can move beyond the win-lose environment of litigation to the full range of options available to avoid disputes and solve our clients' problems. By making this commitment, we have the opportunity to add substantial value both to our clients and to our profession. And by ensuring that business executives remain full owners and partners in these endeavors—and stepping aside when that is the best way forward—we can get the best results in a cost-effective manner and thereby increase respect and appreciation for the profession as a whole.

Bibliography

Selected Readings

This relatively short bibliography is a highly curated selection of publications and websites that address various topics in this book, and which the authors have turned to for guidance and ideas. The selection includes some of their own publications, which summarize their ideas and experience. The websites of the major domestic and international ADR providers often are very useful sources of information.

Alliance Management

The Association of Strategic Alliance Professionals. https://www.strategic-alliances.org.

Dispute Resolution Boards

Dispute Resolution Board Foundation. https://www.drb.org.

International Chamber of Commerce Dispute Board. https://iccwbo.org/dispute-resolution-services/dispute-boards/.

Early Neutral Evaluation

Brazil, Wayne D. *Early Neutral Evaluation*. American Bar Association, 2012.

Facilitation

Essential Partners. https://whatisessential.org.

Vantage Partners. https://www.vantagepartners.com/about/leadership.

Mediation

Bernard, Phyllis and Bryant Garth. *Dispute Resolution Ethics: A Comprehensive Guide*. American Bar Association, 2002.

Bush, Robert A. Baruch and Joseph P. Folger. *The Promise of Mediation: Responding to Conflict through Empowerment and Recognition*. Jossey-Bass Publishers, 1994.

Cooley, John W. *Mediation Advocacy*. National Institute for Trial Advocacy, 1996.

Galton, Eric. *Representing Clients in Mediation*. Texas Lawyer Press, 1994.

Golann, Dwight. *Mediating Legal Disputes: Effective Strategies for Lawyers and Mediators*. Little, Brown and Company, 1996.

Golann, Dwight. *Sharing a Mediator's Powers: Effective Advocacy in Settlement*. American Bar Association, 2014.

Goldberg, Stephen B., Eric D. Green, and Frank E. A. Sander. *Dispute Resolution*. Little, Brown and Company, 1985.

Henry, James F. and Jethro K. Lieberman. *The Manager's Guide to Resolving Legal Disputes*. Harper & Row, 1985.

Kichaven, Jeff. "Online Mediation One Year In: Personal, Practical Reflections." *ABTL Report* 28 (2021, Fall): 2, 10-12.

Kichaven, Jeff. "Protect Yourself From Biased, Deceptive Mediators: Part 1." *Law360* (2012): 1-6.

Kichaven, Jeff. "Protect Yourself From Biased, Deceptive Mediators: Part 2." *Law360* (2012): 1-6.

Kovach, Kimberlee K. *Mediation: Principles and Practice*. West Publishing Co., 1994.

Little, J. Anderson. *Making Money Talk: How to Mediate Insured Claims and Other Monetary Disputes*. American Bar Association, 2007.

Moore, Christopher W. *The Mediation Process*. Jossey-Bass Publishers, 1986.

Riskin, Leonard L. "The Contemplative Lawyer: On the Potential Contributions of Mindfulness of Mediation to Law Students, Lawyers, and Their Clients." *Harvard Negotiation Law Review* 7 (2002): 1-66.

Rogers, Nancy and Craig A. McEwen. *Mediation: Law, Policy, Practice*. Lawyer's Cooperative Publishing, 1989.

Sussman, Edna and Conna Weiner. "Striving for a 'Bulletproof' Mediation Settlement Agreement." *Alternatives to the High Cost of Litigation* 33 (2015): 49-63.

Williams, Gerald R. *Legal Negotiation and Settlement*. West Publishing Co., 1983.

Van Winkle, John R. *Mediation: A Path Back for the Lost Lawyer*. American Bar Association, 2001.

Weiner, Conna. "Mediating Complex Business Disputes Before Litigation: Making the Most of the Moment." *The Resolver* (2018, Spring): 9-13. Accessible at publications tab in www.jamsadr.com/weiner.

Weiner, Conna. "Is Contractually Required Mediation of Business Disputes a Waste of Time?" *New York Law Journal* 261 (2019). https://www.law.com/newyorklawjournal/2019/05/14/is-contractually-required-mediation-of-complex-business-disputes-a-waste-of-time/. Accessible at publications tab in www.jamsadr.com/weiner.

Diversity in Mediation

American Bar Association Resolution 105. Resolution, report, summary, and action steps. https://www.americanbar.org/groups/dispute_resolution/resources/aba-resolution-105/.

International Mediation

European Union Mediation Directive (the Singapore Convention). https://eur-lex.europa.eu/legal-content/EN/TXT/?qid=1539262656162&uri=CELEX:32008L0052.

Linklaters. "Commercial Mediation: A Global Review." https://www.linklaters.com/en/insights/publications/commercial-mediation-a-global-review/commercial-mediation-a-global-review.

Negotiation

The discussion in chapter 5 about the barriers in negotiations is based in part upon the authors' personal experiences in mediation, as well as research in the field. There are a number of important works that examine similar barriers in negotiations from a more theoretical perspective. Among these are Robert Mnookin's diagnostic approach, which identifies four classic barriers to agreement: cognitive, strategic, principal-agent, and reactive devaluation. See Robert H. Mnookin, "Why Negotiations Fail: An Exploration of Barriers to Resolution of Conflict" (*Ohio State Journal on Dispute Resolution* 8, 1993). Christopher Moore, in "Circle of Conflict," identifies conflicts as emanating from data, interests, structure, values, or relationships. See Christopher W. Moore, *The Mediation Process* (Jossey-Bass Publishers, 1986).

Any critical analysis of the negotiation process must also recognize the effectiveness of a problem-solving approach, in contrast to a more competitive approach focused on winning. Carrie Menkel-Meadow addresses the benefits to be achieved by parties crafting solutions to expand the available resources and meet the needs of the parties. See Carrie Menkel-Meadow, "Toward Another View of Legal Negotiation: The Structure of Problem Solving" (*UCLA Law Review* 31, 1984).

Gerry Williams's analytical approach identifies the five steps to recovering from conflict—denial, acceptance, sacrifice, leap of faith, and renewal. Drawing upon the literature in law, psychology, anthropology, and related disciplines, Williams discusses the potential for the disputants to be transformed by the process. See Gerald R. Williams, "Negotiation as a Healing Process" (*Journal of Dispute Resolution* 1, 1996).

Daniel Kahneman's important book on the way our minds work is very useful in thinking about negotiation, and we discuss several of his foundational concepts. See Daniel Kahneman, *Thinking, Fast and Slow* (Farrar, Straus and Giroux, 2011). See generally chapters 2 and 3.

These and other resources are listed below.

Bazerman, Max H. and Margaret A. Neale. *Negotiating Rationally*. Free Press, 1992.

Ertel, Danny. "Getting Past Yes: Negotiating as if Implementation Mattered." *Harvard Business Review Magazine* (November 2004).

Ertel, Danny and Mark Gordon. *The Point of the Deal: How to Negotiate When Yes is Not Enough*. Harvard Business School Press, 2007.

Fisher, Roger. "Negotiating Power." *American Behavioral Scientist* 27 (1983).

Fisher, Roger and William Ury. *Getting To Yes: Negotiating Agreement Without Giving In*. Houghton Mifflin Co., 1981.

Guthrie, Chris, Jeffrey J. Rachlinski, and Andrew J. Wistrich. "Inside the Judicial Mind." *Cornell Law Review* 86 (2001): 4.

Kahneman, Daniel. *Thinking, Fast and Slow*. Farrar, Straus and Giroux, 2011. See generally chapters 2 and 3.

Menkel-Meadow, Carrie. "Toward Another View of Legal Negotiation: The Structure of Problem Solving." *UCLA Law Review* 31 (1984):754.

Mnookin, Robert H. "Why Negotiations Fail: An Exploration of Barriers to Resolution of Conflict." *Ohio State Journal on Dispute Resolution* 8 (1993): 235.

Mnookin, Robert H., Scott R. Peppet, and Andrew S. Tulumello. *Beyond Winning: Negotiating to Create Value in Deals and Disputes*. Harvard University Press, 2000.

Shell, Richard G. *Bargaining for Advantage*. Viking Penguin, 1999.

Ury, William. *Getting Past No: Negotiating with Difficult People*. Bantam Books, 1991.

Williams, Gerald R. "Negotiation as a Healing Process." *Journal of Dispute Resolution* 1 (1996).

Online Dispute Resolution

European Union Online Dispute Resolution. https://ec.europa.eu/consumers/odr/main/?event=main.trader.register.

Katsh, Ethan and Janet Rifkind. *Online Dispute Resolution: Resolving Conflicts in Cyberspace*. John Wiley & Sons, 2001.

Katsh, Ethan et al., eds. *Online Dispute Resolution: Theory and Practice*. Eleven International Publishing, 2012.

Rule, Colin. "Designing a Global Online Dispute Resolution System: Lessons Learned from eBay." *University of St. Thomas Law Journal* 13 (2017): 354.

Rule, Colin. *Online Dispute Resolution for Business*. John Wiley & Sons, 2002.

Smartsettle. Algorithm-assisted online negotiation, founded by Ernie Theissen. https://www.smartsettle.com.

The National Center for Technology & Dispute Resolution. University of Massachusetts, Amherst. https://odr.info/.

General ADR, including Provider and General Websites

These websites contain many useful resources, including clause template language and guidelines, related not only to mediation but to many forms of dispute resolution.

American Arbitration Association
www.adr.org
American College of Civil Trial Mediators
www.acctm.org
CPR Institute for Dispute Resolution
www.cpradr.org
International Academy of Mediators
www.iamed.org
JAMS
www.jamsadr.com
Silicon Valley Arbitration and Mediation Center
https://svamc.org/

U.S. Government
U.S. Department of Justice
Office of Dispute Resolution
www.usdoj.gov/odr

Current Developments/Issues
American Bar Association
Section of Dispute Resolution
www.abanet.org/dispute
Mediate.com
www.mediate.com

International (in addition to websites above that also address international issues)
American Arbitration Association
www.adr.org
Centre for Effective Dispute Resolution (CEDR)
www.cedr.co.uk
International Chamber of Commerce
www.iccwbo.org
London Court of International Arbitration
www.lcia-arbitration.com/lcia
World Intellectual Property Organization
Arbitration and Mediation Center
www.arbiter.wipo.int

Labor
U.S. Department of Labor
www.dol.gov
National Labor Relations Board
www.nlrb.gov

Construction
Associated General Contractors
www.agc.org
National Association of Home Builders
www.nahb.com

Healthcare
American Health Lawyers Association
Alternative Dispute Resolution Service
www.healthlawyers.com

Index

L

M